Joan Fisher's Guide to
Needlecraft

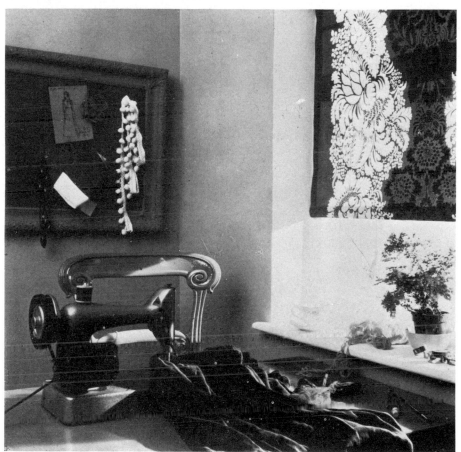

Ward Lock Ltd, London

Guide to Needlecraft

by Joan Fisher

ISBN 0 7063 1353 4
Published by
Ward Lock Limited
Designed and produced by
Trewin Copplestone Publishing Ltd, London
© Trewin Copplestone Publishing Ltd 1972
Colour and monochrome origination by
City Engraving Co (Hull) Ltd
Printed in Great Britain by Sir Joseph Causton
& Sons Ltd, London and Eastleigh
Second impression, 1973

CONTENTS

INTRODUCTION

A needle and a length of yarn . . . basic materials perhaps, but to the needlewoman they can be as expressive and as individual as palette and brush are to an artist, pen and paper to a writer.

And the results can be as fascinating and as wide-ranging. A child's simple embroidery worked in a single stitch, an ambitious and intricate tapestry wall hanging, a cobwebby lace edging, a multicoloured Fair Isle pullover . . . each is achieved with just needle and thread.

To be skilled with a needle has long been a hallmark of accomplishment for young ladies. In the 17th century, when the King of Siam asked King James I to provide him with an English wife, he was offered a young lady described as being of excellent parts for 'music, her needle and good discourse'.

Perhaps a skill in needlecraft is no longer a prerequisite of wifely prowess, but the attraction of making things to wear or to decorate our homes has never really changed. There is still, and no doubt always will be, a great satisfaction in producing fine traditional embroideries. On the other hand, an ability to knit, crochet or dressmake can bring instant fashion right to your fingertips, and give you the pleasure of making and wearing low-cost garments in colours and styles tailormade to suit you perfectly. And, on a practical level, an understanding of sewing techniques will help you to make elegant soft furnishings to enhance your home.

This book offers an introduction to the basic needlecraft subjects: knitting, crochet, embroidery, needlepoint tapestry, sewing, macramé and soft furnishings. The age-old craft of macramé involves no needles and no stitches . . . just yarn and knots. But almost every trade and profession boasts its own range of knots: the surgeon has his knots, so has the gardener, and so has the seaman . . . The decorative macramé knot is the needlewoman's knot, and for this reason justifies its place here.

Clear instructions in the techniques of each craft are followed in every chapter – except soft furnishings – by a number of attractive designs to make up, showing how these techniques can be used to best advantage.

This book should inspire you to create with needle and thread many beautiful things, and should open doors to a world of creative satisfaction and rewarding self-expression.

JOAN FISHER

Chapter one
KNITTING

Knitting has long been a popular craft with women of all ages – and many men as well.

Nowadays with a vast range of exciting new and novelty yarns available, as well as traditional wools in all weights, plus easy-care machine-washable synthetics, it is possible to knit almost any garment for women, babies, children and men. The basic techniques of the craft are simple and quick to master, but practice is needed to achieve evenness and to work to speed. If you are

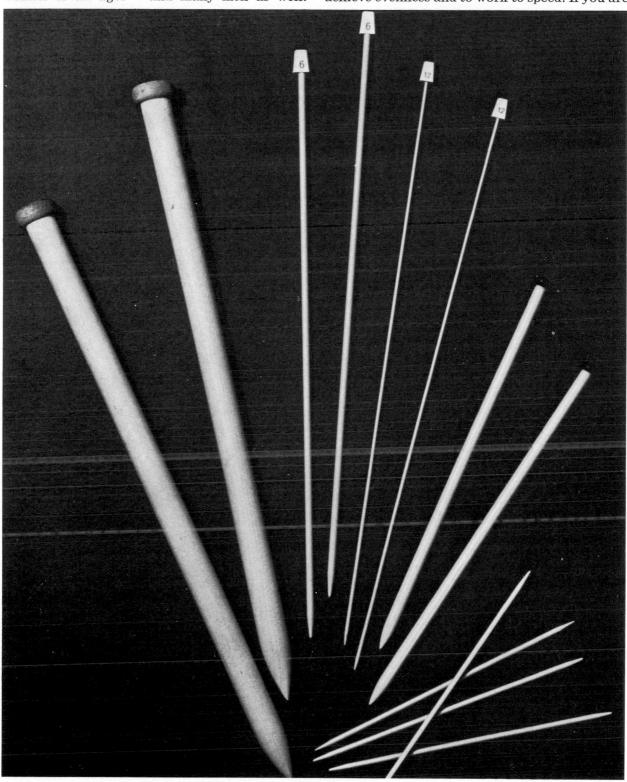

a beginner, then choose straightforward small items to start with, and gradually progress to more ambitious designs.

EQUIPMENT

The only two essentials for knitting are a pair of needles and a ball of yarn, though a few additional items will help to make life easier.

Needles

Knitting needles are available in various thicknesses, the sizes being denoted by a series of numbers (see chart below). In the British range of sizes, the lower numbers indicate the thickest needles, the high numbers the fine needles. In the USA the system is in reverse, with the high numbers used for thick needles, low numbers for fine ones. Needles may be made of metal, nylon, plastic or wood, and each size is usually available in a choice of lengths. Which length you choose is a matter of personal preference, although a pattern involving a great number of stitches will be more comfortably worked on long needles. Needles should always be clean, smooth and rigid – never use needles which show an inclination to bend easily. It is well worth while always buying the best-quality needles.

GUIDE TO KNITTING NEEDLE SIZES

BRITISH SIZES	CONTINENTAL SIZES	USA SIZES
14	2	0
13	–	–
12	2.50	1
11	3.00	2
10	3.25	3
–	3.50	4
9	4.00	5
8	4.40	6
7	4.75	7
6	5.00	8
5	5.50	9
4	6.00	10
3	7.00	10½
2	8.00	11
1	9.25	13

Yarns

Wool is the traditional yarn for knitting, but there are many excellent synthetic yarns available now, and also mixtures of wool and synthetics which combine the advantages of each. Cotton yarns are good for knitting summer clothes and babies' wear. Most yarns are available in different thicknesses – 2, 3 or 4-ply, double knitting and so on; your pattern will tell you which to use. As the colour of yarn may vary slightly between dye lots, it is important to buy all the yarn you need for a particular design from the same dye lot (a dye lot number is usually marked on the label of each ball). Most shops will put the yarn aside for you for a period of time so you can buy it a few balls at a time if you do not want to buy the whole amount at the beginning.

Cable needles

These are very short needles with points at both ends used for taking stitches to the front or back of the knitting when working a cable pattern. Choose a cable needle as near as possible to the size of the needles being used for the main pattern.

Stitch holder

Frequently a pattern will instruct you to leave a number of stitches aside while others are knitted, then the first stitches are returned to later. Some patterns suggest keeping these stitches on a spare needle until required, but a stitch holder is more satisfactory as there is then no danger of any stitches slipping off and unravelling. Small numbers of stitches can be kept on a safety pin.

Also useful

A **tape measure** – to measure the garment as you knit it.
A **row counter** – this is a small tube placed on the end of the needle; it has numbers which you turn up after each row to keep a count of the number of rows worked.
A **crochet hook** – to work a crochet border round a finished knitted garment; it is also useful for picking up dropped stitches.
For **finishing** garments you will need pins for pinning out to the right size, an iron, ironing board and cloth for pressing, and sewing needles for joining seams.

HOLDING YOUR WORK

Continental methods

In the French method both hands hold the needles from on top. The yarn goes round the little finger, then over the two middle fingers and the first finger. The first finger is used to move the yarn as in the English method. Another method used on the continent has the yarn held by the first finger of the left hand. The needles are held as in the French method, but the yarn goes over the little finger of the left hand, under the middle two fingers than round the first finger.

English method

Pass the yarn round the little finger of the right hand, then take it under the third and middle fingers and then over the first finger. The right-hand needle rests between the thumb and this first finger (like holding a pencil) and the finger stays close to the work. The left-hand needle is held with the fingers and thumb above it and the needle firmly against the palm. During work the left hand pushes the stitches along the needle towards the point, and the right-hand first finger moves the yarn to work each stitch.

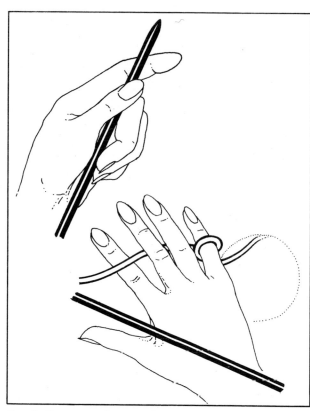

over other yarn and hold loop in left hand.

Now take a needle in your right hand, put it through the loop and with it draw through the main yarn from the ball, thus making a loop on the needle itself. Pull the yarn end to draw loop tight.

Hold the needle with the loop on it in the right hand with the main yarn coming from the ball at the back; hold other yarn in left hand under all four fingers. Take this yarn round left thumb clockwise close to the needle. Insert point of needle into loop on thumb, pass main yarn from

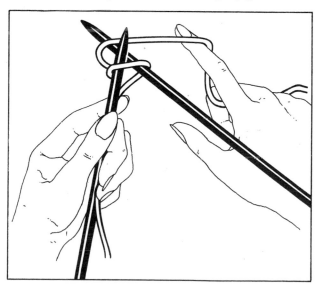

ball under needle point, then with needle draw yarn through loop and let loop on thumb slip off. Pull the yarn gently to draw stitch tight. Continue making stitches in this way until the required number is reached.

Left-handed workers

If you are left-handed, then the above procedures are merely reversed – i.e. for the English method, the left hand controls the yarn, and the right hand controls the stitches.

CASTING ON

Thumb method

Undo a length of yarn from the ball – about three times the finished length required.

Make a slip loop: hold yarn between thumb and first finger of left hand; take yarn from ball in right hand and make a loop by taking main yarn

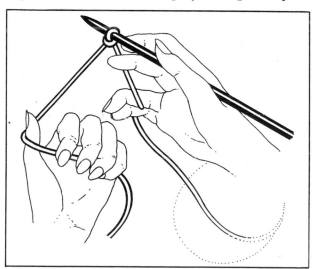

Two-needle method

Draw a short length of yarn from ball then make a slip loop as described in the thumb method above. Put needle with slip loop on it into left hand with main yarn at front.

Taking second needle in right hand, insert this needle into loop from left to right, pass main

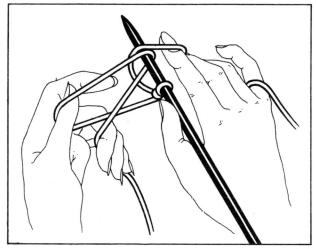

yarn under point of right-hand needle and then with this needle draw main yarn through loop to form a new loop on needle. Transfer this new loop to left-hand needle which now holds two stitches. Continue in this way until required number of stitches are formed. This method gives a 'looped' edge and if a firm edge is required the first row of knitting must be worked into the backs of the stitches.

Between-stitch method

Begin by making a slip loop and first stitch in a similar way as for the two-needle method above. Now, instead of inserting right-hand needle into stitch on left-hand needle, insert it between the two stitches, then complete stitch as for two-needle method. Continue in this way for length required. This method gives a twisted edge.

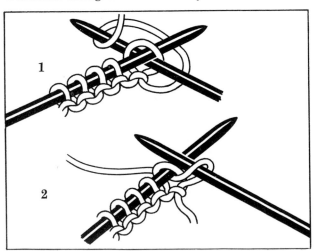

STITCHES

Knit stitch

Hold the needle with your cast-on stitches in your left hand and the empty needle and main yarn in your right hand (or vice versa if you are left-handed). Insert right-hand needle into first stitch on left-hand needle from left to right, main yarn at back of work, then take yarn under point of right-hand needle (diagram 1). With right-hand needle pull main yarn through stitch to form a loop on right-hand needle (diagram 2) and let loop on left-hand needle slip off. One stitch has been knitted on to right-hand needle. Continue along row in this way.

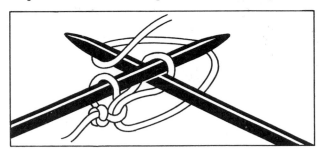

Purl stitch

Hold the needle with your cast-on stitches in your left hand and the empty needle and main yarn in right hand. Insert right-hand needle into first stitch from right to left, main yarn at front of work. Take yarn over and then under point of right-hand needle. Turn right-hand needle away from you to draw loop through on to needle and then drop loop from left-hand needle. Continue along row in this way.

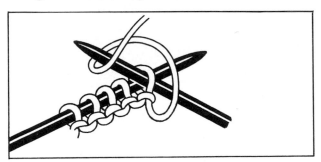

INCREASING

At the beginning or end of a row increases of several stitches can be made by casting on. Increases of a single stitch made by one of the following methods are usually worked within the main body of the work, and not at the end of a row.

Work twice into one stitch

This is the most usual method. Start to knit or purl the stitch in the usual way but do not drop the loop from the left-hand needle; now insert right-hand needle into back of loop from right to left for a knit stitch or from left to right for a purl stitch, and work into it again. The diagram, below shows a knit stitch being worked into for the second time.

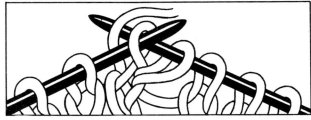

Yarn round needle or yarn over needle

This method of increasing leaves a small hole in

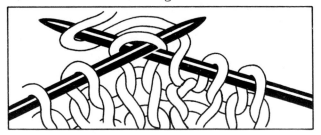

the knitting so is usually used in lacy patterns. Between the two knit stitches the yarn is brought forward to the front of the work and over needle to the back again before knitting the next stitch.

After a knit stitch and before a purl stitch the yarn is brought forward under the needle, taken back over the needle and round to the front again under the needle.

After a purl stitch and before a knit stitch the yarn is taken over the needle to the back.

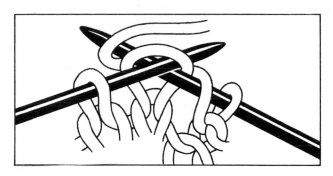

Between two purl stitches the yarn is taken over the needle to the back then under the needle to the front again.
In every case the strand which goes over the needle is worked as a stitch on the next row.

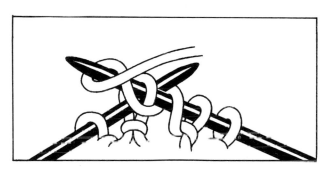

Lifting loop from previous row

Another method of making an extra stitch is to lift the loop lying between the last stitch and the next stitch on to the left-hand needle and then to knit it through the back of the loop.

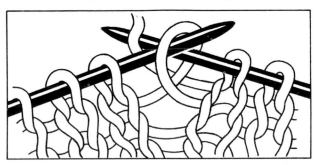

DECREASING

At the beginning of a row decreases of several stitches can be made by casting off (see below). Decreases of one or two stitches made by any of the following methods are usually worked within the main body of the work and not at the end of a row.

Working two stitches together

Two stitches, sometimes three, are knitted or purled together as one stitch. When two stitches are knitted together the decreased stitch slopes to the right, so if lines of decreases are being worked at each end of the work – such as on a skirt – decreases at the end of the row are often worked by knitting two stitches together through the backs of the loops as this makes the decreased stitch slope to the left. The reverse happens when two stitches are purled together.

Pass slipped stitch over

This is worked by slipping one stitch on to the right-hand needle without working into it, then knitting the next stitch; the slipped stitch is then passed over the knitted stitch and dropped off the needle.

CASTING OFF

Never cast off too tightly, unless the pattern specifically instructs you to do so, as there is much less 'give' in this last row than in ordinary knitting.
Work the first two stitches of the row in the usual way, keeping pattern correct. With the point of the left-hand needle lift the first stitch worked over the second stitch and let it fall. Work another stitch on to the right-hand needle then lift the first stitch over the second again. Work all along the row until only one stitch remains. Draw up this stitch to make it a long one, remove needle, break yarn and thread yarn end through stitch. Draw up tightly.

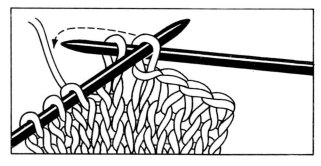

TENSION

Every pattern gives a tension measurement which refers to the number of stitches and rows which should be equal to one square inch for that particular pattern. Different sizes of needles will give different tension measurements with the same yarn. To achieve the correct size of finished article it is essential to work to the tension given in the pattern. Before starting work on any garment test your tension by working a small square, of 3 or 4 in., using the yarn and needle size recommended by the pattern, and the correct stitch pattern. Press this square then mark off with pins a 2-in. square in the middle of it. Count the number of stitches and rows in this square and check them with the tension given in the pattern. If the stitches and rows are fewer than those given, try again with needles a size smaller; if they are too many, try again with needles a size larger. Only start to knit the garment when you have found the right needles to achieve the correct tension.

JOINING YARN

If possible start a new ball of yarn at the beginning of a row. Tie the old and new yarn ends in a knot and darn in the ends later. If a join cannot be avoided, unravel the end of the old ball for 2 in. or so. Cut away half the strands. Do the same at the start of the new ball, then twist these two ends together, thus making the same thickness as normal.

DROPPED STITCHES

Your crochet hook will be useful here, though a knitting needle will do if you do not have one. Slip the hook or needle into the dropped stitch, then work up the loops of each row one at a time, as shown in the diagram below. This is not such an arduous task as it sounds!

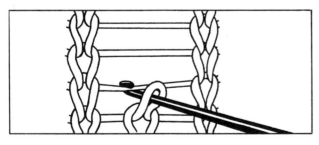

MAKING UP

When you have finished knitting the various parts of a garment, they then have to be sewn together to make the complete design. This is an important stage, for often a garment which has been neatly and carefully knitted is spoiled by careless making-up. First the individual pieces have to be pressed: if specific instructions are given in the pattern, follow these as different yarns require different treatments. Wool is usually pressed with a warm iron over a damp cloth; synthetics with a cool iron over a dry cloth. A rib pattern is not usually pressed at all as it loses its stretchiness. Before pressing, pin out each piece of work to its correct measure-

ments, with wrong side up, then press in the appropriate way. Sew in any loose ends of yarn, and join seams using a large-eyed needle threaded with the same yarn as used for knitting. Your pattern will usually tell you which stitch to use for joining seams, but generally a backstitch is used for seams such as side, sleeve or shoulder, while an overcast stitch is used for joining edgings to the main work.

Grafting

This is a process by which two pieces of knitting can be joined without casting off and without making a seam. Place the two needles with the stitches on them together and then using a tapestry needle and length of yarn, 'sew' a new row of knitted stitches between the two groups. The diagram below clearly shows how this is done, and how two stitches are slipped off each needle alternately. The diagram below shows grafting being worked in a stocking stitch pattern, but grafting may of course be worked in any stitch pattern.

CIRCULAR KNITTING

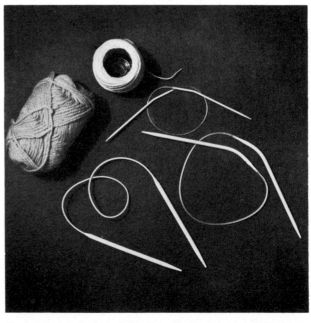

Sometimes it is wished to knit in a continuous seamless tube – for a sock or polo collar, for example. This can be done either by using a set of four needles with points at both ends or one long flexible circular needle with points at both ends. With four needles, it is best to cast all stitches on to one needle and then divide them among three needles – the fourth is used for the knitting. Work the first and last stitches of each needle tightly to avoid a gap. When working in rounds in this way, remember the right side is facing on every round. When working with a circular needle it is important to choose the correct length of needle for the pattern you are working. Stitches should reach from point to point on the needle without stretching.

SIMPLE PATTERNS

Stocking stitch. This consists of one row of all knit stitches and one row of all purl stitches worked alternately. It gives a smooth surface on the right (knit) side. Sometimes the reverse side is used as the right side and this is called reversed stocking stitch.

Garter stitch. Every row is a knit row. An elastic, ridged piece of work results.

Ribbing. Usually each row consists of one stitch knit followed by one stitch purl all along, though two knit stitches and two purl, or even more, are often used. One the second row stitches which were knitted on the first row are purled and vice versa.

Example of single rib (k.1, p.1) pattern.

Example of double rib (k.2, p.2) pattern.

Moss stitch. This is worked in a similar way to single rib, but stitches which were knitted on first row are again knitted on second row, and purl stitches are purled. Double moss stitch is two stitches knitted followed by two stitches purled.

Fair Isle. When two colours of yarn are worked on the same row, it is easiest to hold one colour in the left hand and one in the right. This takes a little mastering, but it is worth while if you intend to do a lot of colour work. Otherwise, you can pick up each yarn in turn in your right hand as usual. If each colour is used for only a few stitches, the yarn not in use is carried behind the work (diagram 1, page 12), with yarns crossed at each change of colour. If more stitches are being worked in each colour, the yarn not in use should be woven through the back of the stitches (see diagram 2).

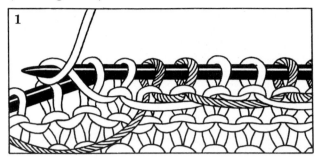

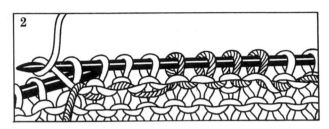

ABBREVIATIONS

The following are the abbreviations normally used in knitting patterns.

alt.	alternate
beg.	beginning
cont.	continue
dec.	decreas(e) (ed) (ing)
foll.	following
g.st.	garter stitch
in.	inch(es)
inc.	increas(e) (ed) (ing)
k.	knit
p.	purl
patt.	pattern
p.s.s.o.	pass slipped stitch over
rem.	remain(ing) (der)
rep.	repeat
st.	stitch
st.st.	stocking stitch
t.b.l.	through back of loop
tog.	together
y.b.	yarn back
y.f.	yarn forward
y.o.n.	yarn over needle
y.r.n.	yarn round needle

Pattern sizes. If a pattern gives a range of different sizes, then normally instructions are given in size order, with the different instructions relating to larger sizes in brackets. Where only one set of figures occurs this refers to all sizes.

THE PATTERNS

Man's Aran sweater
Illustrated in colour on page 20

MATERIALS. 18 (19, 21, 22) 50-gram balls of Mahony's Blarney Bainin (USA: Blarneyspun) wool. One pair each Nos. 7, 9 and 10 knitting needles (USA: sizes 7, 5 and 3). A cable needle.

MEASUREMENTS. To fit chest size 36/38 (39/41, 42/44, 45/47) in.; sleeve seam 19 (19½, 20, 20) in.; centre back length 26 (27, 28, 29) in.

TENSION. One patt. of 12 sts. over small size patt. measures 2 in.; 7½ rows to 1 in. over patt.

ABBREVIATIONS. See left; C.4 B. (or C.4 F.), cable 4 back (or front) thus — slip next 2 sts. on to cable needle, leave at back (or front) of work, k.2, then k.2 from cable needle; k.f.b. (or p.f.b.), knit (or purl) into front and back of next st.

BACK
With No. 10 needles cast on 93 (101, 109, 117) sts. Work in rib.
1st row (right side): k.2, * p.1, k.1; rep. from * to last st., k.1.
2nd row: k.1, * p.1, k.1; rep. from * to end.
Rep. these 2 rows 6 times more, then the first row again.
Inc. row (wrong side): k.3, * p.3, p.f.b., p.3, k.1 (1, 2, 2), k.f.b., k.1 (2, 2, 3); rep. from * to last 10 sts., p.3, p.f.b., p.3, k.3: 110 (118, 126, 134) sts.
Change to No. 7 needles and patt.
1st row: k.2, * p.1, k.8, p.1, k.2 (3, 4, 5); rep. from * to last 12 sts., p.1, k.8, p.1, k.2.
2nd row: k.3, * p.8, k.4 (5, 6, 7); rep. from * to last 11 sts., p.8, k.3.
Rep. these 2 rows once.
5th row: k.2, * p.1, C.4 B., C.4 F., p.1, k.2 (3, 4, 5); rep. from * to last 12 sts., p.1, C.4 B., C.4 F., p.1, k.2.
6th row: as 2nd.
Rep. first and 2nd rows once.
9th row: as 5th.
10th row: as 2nd.
Rep. first and 2nd rows twice.
15th row: k.2, * p.1, C.4 F., C.4 B., p.1, k.2 (3, 4, 5); rep. from * to last 12 sts., p.1, C.4 F., C.4 B., p.1, k.2.
16th row: as 2nd.
Rep. first and 2nd rows once.
19th row: as 15th.
20th row: as 2nd.
These 20 rows form one patt. Continue in patt. but inc. 1 st. at both ends of row when work measures 7 in. and 11 in. from beg., keeping extra sts. at sides in g.st. Continue on these 114 (122, 130, 138) sts. without shaping until work measures 17½ (18, 18½, 19) in. from beg.

Armhole Shaping. Cast off 4 (5, 6, 7) sts. at beg. of next 4 rows and 4 sts. at beg. of next 2 rows: 90 (94, 98, 102) sts. remain. Continue in patt. with 4 (3, 2, 1) sts. in g.st. at each end of row, until work measures 25 (26, 27, 28) in. from beg., ending with a wrong-side row.

Shoulder and Neck Shaping. 1st row: cast off 5 (6, 7, 8), patt. until there are 33 sts. on right-hand needle, leave these sts. on a spare needle for right back, continue along row, cast off 14 (16, 18, 20) sts., then patt. to end. Continue on the 38 (39, 40, 41) sts. now remaining on needle for left back.
2nd row: cast off 5 (6, 7, 8), patt. back to neck edge.
** **3rd row:** cast off 4, patt. to end.

4th row: cast off 7, patt. back to neck edge. Rep. last 2 rows once, then 3rd row again. Cast off remaining 7 sts. **
With wrong side facing, rejoin wool to inner edge of right back sts. Complete as given for left back from ** to **.

FRONT
Work as given for back until you have worked 10 rows less than on back to start of neck shaping, thus ending with a wrong-side row.

Neck and Shoulder Shaping. 1st row: patt. 40 (41, 42, 43) and leave these sts. on a spare needle for left front, continue along row, cast off 10 (12, 14, 16) sts., then patt. to end. Continue on the 40 (41, 42, 43) sts. now remaining on needle for right front and work 1 row straight. *** Cast off 3 sts. at beg. of next row, then dec. 1 st. at same edge on next 8 rows. Now cast off for shoulders 5 (6, 7, 8) sts. at beg. of next row, then dec. 1 st. at neck edge on following row. Cast off 7 sts. at beg. of next row and dec. 1 st. at neck edge on following row. Rep. last 2 rows once. Cast off remaining 7 sts. *** With wrong side facing, rejoin wool to inner edge of left front sts. Complete as for right front from *** to ***.

SLEEVES (make 2 alike)
With No. 10 needles cast on 53 (57, 61, 65) sts. and work first 16 rows exactly as for back; when the inc. row has been worked you will have 62 (66, 70, 74) sts.
Change to No. 7 needles and work in patt. as given for back but when first patt. is completed, inc. 1 st. at both ends of first, 7th and 14th rows of every patt. until there are 88 (94, 100, 106) sts. taking extra sts. into patt. When all incs. are completed you will have 3 sts. in g.st. at each end. Continue without shaping until work measures 19 (19½, 20, 20) in. from beg. Place marker loops of contrast wool at each end of last row, then work 16 (19, 21, 24) rows straight.

To Shape Top. Cast off 4 sts. at beg. of next 4 rows and 4 (5, 6, 7) sts. at beg. of next 2 rows. Rep. last 6 rows once. Cast off 6 sts. at beg. of next 2 rows and 6 (7, 8, 9) sts. at beg. of next 2 rows: 16 sts. remain for all sizes. Continue on these sts. in patt. with the cable in centre and 3 sts. in g.st. at each edge until this strip is long enough to fit along front shoulder edge. Cast off.

NECKBAND
With No. 9 needles cast on 127 (131, 135, 139) sts. and work in rib as on welt for 4 rows. Change to No. 10 needles and work 8 rows. Change back to No. 9 needles and work 4 rows. Cast off ribwise.

TO COMPLETE
Do not press. First pin sleeves in place matching markers to beg. of armhole casting-off, pinning straight rows of sleeves above markers to armhole casting-off, shaped edges of sleeves to sides of armholes and sides of extension strip to shoulder edges. The cast-off edge of extension strips forms part of neckline. Remove markers and sew sleeves in place backstitching these and all seams. Press seams lightly on wrong side with warm iron and damp cloth taking care not to stretch patt. Join side and sleeve seams and press. Join ends of neckband. With right sides together and join level with left back shoulder seam, sew cast-on edge of neckband to neck edges, easing in neckline to fit band. Press seam using point of iron so as not to flatten rib. Fold band in half to inside and slip-st. cast-off edge to previous seam.

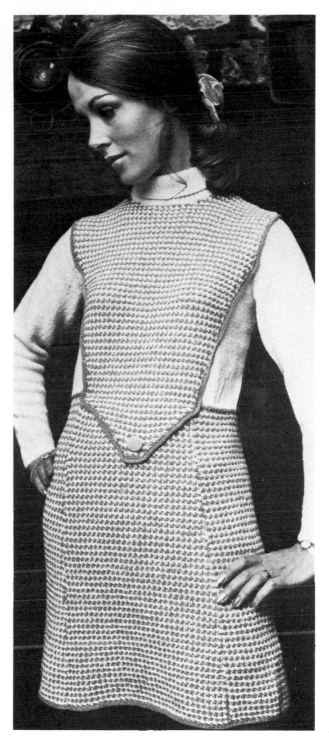

Two-colour dress

MATERIALS. 13 (14, 15) oz. Emu Super Crepe in main shade and 7 (8, 9) oz. in a contrasting shade (or any 4-ply yarn to give tension indicated below). One pair each No. 9, No. 10, No. 11 and No. 12 knitting needles (USA sizes 5, 3, 2 and 1). One crochet hook International Standard Size 3.00. One medium button.

MEASUREMENTS. To fit bust size 34 (36, 38) in. and hip size 36 (38, 40) in.; length 35 (35½, 36) in.; length of sleeve seam 17 in.

TENSION. 17 sts. and 20 rows to 2 in. over tweed patt. with No. 9 needles.

ABBREVIATIONS. See page 12; M., main shade; C., contrasting shade.

SKIRT FRONT AND BACK PANELS (make 2 alike)
With No. 9 needles and C. cast on 103 (106, 109) sts. and p. 1 row. Join M. and work in tweed patt.
1st row: with M. k.1, * sl.1 purlwise, y.f. (to make 1), sl.1 purlwise, k.1, pass first slipped st. over foll. 3 sts.; rep. from * to end.
2nd row: with M., p. to end taking care to keep sts. in correct order, with groups of 1 st. M., 1.C., 1 M.
3rd row: with C., * sl.1 purlwise, y.f. (to make 1), sl.1 purlwise, k.1, pass first slipped st. over foll. 3 sts.; rep. from * to last st., k.1.
4th row: with C., p. to end, working sts. in correct order, with groups of 1 C., 1 M., 1 C.
These 4 rows form the tweed patt. Work 24 rows more straight, then dec. 1 st. at each end of next and every foll. 10th row until 83 (86, 89) sts. remain. Work 5 rows straight then dec. 1 st. at each end of next and every foll. 8th row until 69 (72, 75) sts. remain.
Cont. straight until Panel measures 20 in. from beg., ending with a wrong-side row. With C., p.1 row. Cast off.

SKIRT SIDE PANELS (make 2 alike)
Work as Skirt Front and Back Panels but do not cast off. Leave sts. on st. holder.

BODICE CENTRE BACK
With No. 9 needles and C. cast on 7 (10, 13) sts. and p. 1 row. Join M. and work in tweed patt. as given for Skirt, inc. 1 st. at each end of 3rd and every foll. row until there are 69 (72, 75) sts., working inc. sts. in st.st. until group is formed that can be worked in patt. Place coloured markers at each end of last row. Work 1 row straight, then inc. 1 st. at each end of next and every foll. 4th row until there are 121 (124, 127) sts., ending with a wrong-side row. Place coloured markers at each end of last row.**
Cont. straight until work measures 5 (5½, 6) in. from second coloured markers, ending with a wrong-side row.

Shape Shoulders. Cast off 13 (12, 13) sts. at beg. of next 2 rows, then 12 (13, 13) sts. at beg. of next 4 rows. Cast off rem. 47 (48, 49) sts.

BODICE CENTRE FRONT
Work as Bodice Centre Back to **. Cont. straight until work

measures 3 (3½, 4) in. from second coloured markers, ending with a wrong-side row.

Shape Neck. Next row: patt. 51 (52, 53) sts., cast off 19 (20, 21) sts., patt. to end.
Cont. on last sts. only. Work 1 row.
Now cast off 3 sts. at neck edge on next and foll. 2 alt. rows, then dec. 1 st. at same edge on every alt. row until 37 (38, 39) sts. remain. Cont. straight if necessary until armhole measures same as Back to shoulder, ending at armhole edge.

Shape Shoulder. Cast off 13 (12, 13) sts. at beg. of next row, then cast off 12 (13, 13) sts. at beg. of foll. 2 alt. rows. Join yarn to rem. sts. and work to match first side of neck, reversing shapings.

BODICE SIDE PANELS (make 2 alike)
Return to 69 (72, 75) Side Panel sts. on st. holder. Break C. and cont. in M. only. With No. 10 needles work in k.1, p.1 rib.
For size 34 only. 1st row: work twice into first st., rib to end.
For sizes 36 and 38 only. 1st row: rib 15 (7), * work twice into next st., rib 13 (9); rep. from * 2 (5) times more, work twice into next st., rib 14 (7).
For all sizes: 70 (76, 82) sts. Work 2 more rows in k.1, p.1 rib.
Cont. in st.st., beg. with a k. row. Dec. 1 st. at each end of 3rd and every foll. 4th row until 34 (40, 46) sts. remain, ending with a wrong-side row.

Shape Armholes. Next row: k.10 (13, 16), cast off 14 sts., k. to end.
Cont. on last sts. only. Cont. to dec. 1 st. at front edge every 4th row as before, **at the same time** dec. 1 st. at armhole edge on right-side rows until 1 st. remains. Fasten off.
Rejoin yarn to rem. sts. and work to match first side of armhole.

SLEEVES (make 2 alike)
With No. 12 needles and M., cast on 52 (54, 56) sts. and work 1½ in. in k.1, p.1 rib.
Change to No. 10 needles and work in st.st., inc. 1 st. at each end of 5th and every foll. 6th row until there are 90 (94, 98) sts. Cont. straight until work measures 17 in. from beg., ending with a wrong-side row.

Shape Top. Cast off 7 sts. at beg. of next 2 rows, then dec. 1 st. at each end of next row and every alt. row until 56 (58, 60) sts. remain. Now cast off 2 sts. at beg. of next 12 rows, 3 sts. at beg. of next 6 rows and 4 sts. at beg. of next 2 rows. Cast off rem. sts.

TO COMPLETE
Collar. Join left shoulder seam. With right side of work facing, No. 12 needles and M., pick up and k. 49 (50, 51) sts. across back of neck, 27 sts. down left side of front neck, 19 (20, 21) sts. across centre front neck, 27 sts. up right side of front neck. Work in k.1, p.1 rib for 2½ in. Change to No. 11 needles and cont. in k.1, p.1 rib for a further 2 in. Cast off in rib.

To Make Up. Join right shoulder seam. With crochet hook and C., work 2 rows of d.c. firmly round edge of Bodice Centre Front and Back. Join Skirt Front and Skirt Back to Skirt Side Panels. Join Bodice Centre Front and Back to Bodice Side Panels, overlapping crochet edgings, placing lower markers to waist, and second markers to top point of armhole shaping. Catch st. Skirt Front and Back Panels at Bodice Centre Front and Back. Catch st. points of Bodice Centre Front and Centre Back to right side of Skirt. Sew sleeve seams. Insert Sleeves, overlapping crochet edges of Bodice Front and Back. Sew collar side seam with flat seam. With crochet hook and C. work 1 row d.c. firmly round Skirt lower edge. Press seams. Turn collar to right side. Sew on button at front point.

Fair Isle jersey and cap
Also illustrated in colour on page 24

MATERIALS. 6 (7, 8, 10, 11) balls Wendy Double knit Nylonised in main shade, 2 (2, 2, 3, 3,) balls in first contrasting shade and 1 ball in each of 3 more contrasting shades (or any nylonised double knitting yarn to give tension indicated below). One pair each No. 10 and No. 8 knitting needles (USA: sizes 3 and 6).

MEASUREMENTS. Jersey: to fit chest size 24 (26, 28, 30, 32) in.; length 15 (17, 19, 21, 23) in.; length of sleeve seam 9 (10½, 12, 13½, 15) in. (adjustable). **Cap:** To fit an average child's head.

TENSION. 5½ sts. and 7 rows to 1 in. over st.st. with No. 8 needles.

ABBREVIATIONS. See page 12; M., main shade; A., first contrasting shade; B, 2nd contrasting shade; C, 3rd contrasting shade; D., 4th contrasting shade.

JERSEY FRONT
With No. 10 needles and M. cast on 72 (78, 84, 90, 96) sts. and work 3 (3, 2½, 3, 2½) in. in k.1, p.1 rib. Change to No. 8 needles and colour patt. in st.st.
1st row: with M.
2nd row: with M.
3rd row: k. *1 M., 1 B.; rep. from * to end.
4th row: p. *1 A., 1 B.; rep. from * to end.
5th row: with A., k.
6th row: with A., p.
7th row: k. *3A., 3 D.; rep. from * to end.
8th row: p. * 3 D., 3 A.; rep. from * to end.
9th row: as 7th row.
10th row: p. *3 A., 3 C.; rep. from * to end.
11th row: k. *3 C., A 3.; rep. from * to end.
12th row: as 10th row.
13th row: as 5th row.
14th row: as 6th row.
15th row: as 3rd row.
16th row: with M., p.
With M. work 0 (4, 8, 4, 8) rows in st.st., beg. with a k. row. These 16 (20, 24, 20, 24) rows form colour patt. Cont. in patt. Rep. patt. rows 2 (2, 2, 3, 3) times more straight.

Shape Armholes. Keeping patt. always correct, cast off 4 sts. at beg. of next 2 rows. Dec. 1 st. at each end of next 4 (5, 6, 7, 8) rows and foll. alt. row.
Work straight in patt. on rem. 54 (58, 62, 66, 70) sts. until 1 rep. of patt. above beg. armholes has been worked. Cont. in st.st. with M. until 22 (26, 30, 32, 36) rows from beg. of armholes have been worked. Cont. in st.st. with M. **

Shape Neck. Next row: k. 17(18, 19, 20, 21), k.2 tog.; turn.
Patt. another 7 rows on these sts. only, dec. 1 st. at neck edge on next and foll. alt. rows.

Shape Shoulder. Cast off 4 (5, 5, 5, 6) sts. at beg. of next and foll. alt. row, and 6 (5, 6, 7, 6) sts. at beg. of next alt. row. Return to rem. sts., slip first 16 (18, 20, 22, 24) sts. on to a st. holder then work on rem. 19 (20, 21, 22, 23) sts. to match first side of neck, reversing shapings.

JERSEY BACK

Work as Front to **, then cont. straight until Back matches Front to beg. of shoulders.

Shape Shoulders. Cast off 4 (5, 5, 5, 6) sts. at beg. of next 4 rows and 6 (5, 6, 7, 6) sts. at beg. of foll. 2 rows. Leave rem. 26 (28, 30, 32, 34) sts. on st. holder.

JERSEY SLEEVES (make 2 alike)

With No. 10 needles and M., cast on 34 (36, 38, 40, 42) sts. and work 2½ in. in k.1, p.1 rib, inc. 1 st. at each end of last row. Change to No. 8 needles and, beg. with a k. row, cont. in st.st. with M., inc. 1 st. at each end of every 5th row until there are 48 (54, 60, 64, 68) sts. Work straight until Sleeve measures 9 (10½, 12, 13½, 15) in. (or required length) from cast-on edge, ending with a p. row.

Shape Top. Cast off 4 sts. at beg. of next 2 rows, 1 st. at beg. of next 6 rows and 2 sts. at beg. of foll. 10 (12, 14, 16, 18) rows. Cast off.

TO COMPLETE

Polo Neck. Sew right shoulder seam. With right side facing, No. 10 needles and M., beg. at left shoulder and pick up and k. 12 sts. down side of front neck, k. 16 (18, 20, 22, 24) sts. from st. holder, pick up and k. 12 sts. round right side of front neck, k. 26 (28, 30, 32, 34) sts. from st. holder: 66 (70, 74, 78, 82) sts. Work in k.1, p.1 rib. Work 1½ in. with No. 10 needles then 2 in. with No. 8 needles. Cast off loosely in rib.

To Make Up. Press st.st. sections well. Sew left shoulder seam, joining sides of polo neck at same time. Sew side seams and sleeve seams and set in Sleeves. Press st.st. seams.

CAP

With No. 10 needles and M. cast on 90 (96, 102, 108, 114) sts. and work 8 rows in k.1, p.1 rib.
Change to No. 8 needles.
Work the first 16 rows of colour patt. as given for front of Jersey. Begin with a k. row, work 2 (6, 8, 12, 16) rows in st.st. with M. Cont. in st.st. with M.

Shape Crown. 1st row: * k.2 tog., k.11 (12, 13, 14, 15), sl.1, k.1, p.s.s.o.; rep. from * 5 times.
2nd row: p.
3rd row: * k.2 tog., k.9 (10, 11, 12, 13), sl.1, k.1, p.s.s.o.; rep. from * 5 times. Cont. to dec. 12 sts. in same way every k. row until 18 (12, 18, 12, 18) sts. remain, ending with a p. row.
Next row: *k.1, sl.1, k.1, p.s.s.o.; rep. from * to end.
Thread rem. sts. on to 2 strands yarn, pull tight and knot. Press st.st. section well. Sew back seam and press seam. Make a pompon as described on page 141 and sew to centre of Cap.

Cabled sweater

Illustrated in colour opposite

MATERIALS. 15 (16, 17) oz. Emu Scotch 4-ply in main shade and 3 oz. in a contrasting shade (or any 4-ply to give tension indicated below). One pair of No. 10 knitting needles (USA: size 3). One No. 11 and one No. 12 circular knitting needle (USA: sizes 2 and 1). One cable needle.

MEASUREMENTS. To fit bust size 34 (36, 38) in.; length 29 (29½, 30) in.; length of sleeve seam 16½ (17, 17) in.

TENSION. About 9½ sts. to 1 in. when slightly stretched.

ABBREVIATIONS. See page 12; m.1, make 1: pick up loop lying between last and next sts. and k. it t.b.l.; M., main shade; C., contrasting shade.

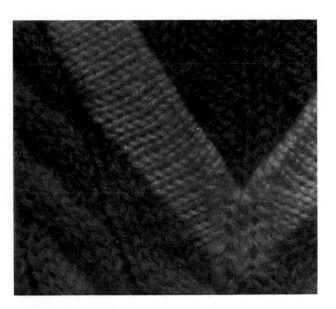

BACK

With No. 10 needles and M., cast on 170 (178, 186) sts.
1st row: p.2, * k.6, p.2; rep. from * to end.
2nd row: k.2, * p.6, k.2; rep. from * to end.
3rd row: p.2, * slip next 3 sts. on to cable needle and leave at front of work, k. next 3 sts., then k. the 3 sts. from cable needle, p.2; rep. from * to end.
4th to 7th rows: rep. 2nd and first rows twice.
8th row: as 2nd row.
These 8 rows form the patt. Cont. straight in patt. until work measures about 7 in. from beg., ending with a 4th patt. row. Join C. and work side panels in st.st. with C. and centre panel in patt. with M., twisting yarns when changing colours.
1st row: with C. k.8, k.2 tog., * k.6, k.2 tog.; rep. from * once (twice, twice), k.6 (0, 2), with M. patt. to last 32 (34, 36) sts., with C. k.6 (0, 2), ** k.2 tog., k.6; rep. from ** once (twice, twice), k.2 tog., k.8.
Work 1 more st. in C. at inner edge of each side panel every row, as 2 p. sts. between cables are worked in C., k. these tog. on right-side row or p. tog. on a wrong-side row. When working a cable row in centre panel, if fewer than 6 sts. are left for cable, always slip 3 sts. on to cable needle and leave at front of work and k. fewer sts. afterwards, so twist is correct. Cont. until the 2 centre p. sts. have been worked in C., ending with a wrong-side row.
Next row: with M., k. across 28 (30, 32) sts., with C. k. to last 28 (30, 32) sts., with M. k. to end.
Next row: with M. k.2, * p.6, k.1, m.1; rep. from * 2 (3, 3) times, p.5 (0, 2), with C. p. to last 28 (30, 32), with M. p.5 (0, 2), ** m.1, k.1, p.6; rep. from ** 2 (3, 3) times, k.2.
Now work side panels in cable patt. with M. and centre panel in st.st. with C., working 1 more st. in M. at inner edge of each side panel every row, and m.1 st. as each p. st. between cables becomes worked in M.
Cont. until all the C. sts. have been worked over and there are 170 (178, 186) sts. once more on needle.***
Work a further 4 in. in patt., with M.

Shape Armholes. Cast off 7 (8, 9) sts. at beg. of next 2 rows, 2 sts. at beg. of next 8 rows then dec. 1 st. at beg. of every row until 126 (130, 134) sts. remain. Cont. straight until armholes measure 7 (7¼, 7½) in.

Shape Shoulders. Cast off 9 (10, 11) sts. at beg. of next 2 rows and 10 sts. at beg. of next 6 rows. Cast off rem. sts.

FRONT

Work as given for Back to ***. Cont. straight in patt. with M. for 2½ in.

Shape Neck. Next row: patt. 85 (89, 93) sts.; turn and leave rem. sts. on a spare needle. Working on the first 85 (89, 93) sts., dec. 1 st. at centre front on next row and every 3rd row 5 times then every foll. 4th row until 24 (25, 26) decs. in all have been made and **at the same time,** when work measures same as Back to armholes end at side edge.

Shape Armhole. Cast off 7 (8, 9) sts. at beg. of next row, 2 sts. at beg. of next 4 alt. rows and 1 st. at beg. of next 7 (8, 9) alt. rows.
Cont. straight at armhole edge still dec. as before at neck edge until 39 (40, 41) sts. remain.
Cont. straight at both edges until work measures same as Back to shoulder, ending at side edge.

Shape Shoulder. Cast off 9 (10, 11) sts. at beg. of next row and 10 sts. at beg. of next 3 alt. rows. Rejoin yarn to rem. sts. and work to match first side of neck, reversing shapings.

SLEEVES (make 2 alike)
With No. 10 needles and M., cast on 74 (74, 82) sts. and work in patt. as given for Back, inc. 1 st. at each end of the 7th row and every foll. 7th row until there are 118 (122, 130) sts., working inc. sts. into patt. Cont. straight until Sleeve measures 16½ (17, 17) in.

Shape top. Cast off 7 (8, 9) sts. at beg. of next 2 rows and 2 sts. at beg. of next 8 rows, then dec. 1 st. at beg. of every row until 50 (50, 54) sts. remain. Cast off 2 sts. at beg. of next 2 rows, 3 (3, 4) sts. at beg. of next 2 rows, 4 (4, 5) sts. at beg. of next 2 rows and 5 sts. at beg. of next 2 rows. Cast off rem. sts.

TO COMPLETE
Neck Border. Join shoulder seams. With No. 11 circular needle and M., and right side facing, pick up and k. 48 (50, 52) sts. across back of neck, pick up and k. 72 (74, 76) sts. down left side of front neck, 1 st. at centre front (mark this st.) and 72 (74, 76) sts. up right side of front neck.
Work in rounds with C.
1st round: k. to within 2 sts. of centre front, sl.1, k.1, p.s.s.o., k. centre st., k.2 tog., k. to end of round.
Rep. the first round 3 times.
Change to No. 12 circular needle and work 3 rounds.
Now inc. each side of centre st.
Next round: k. to centre st., m.1, k. centre st., m.1, k. to end.
Rep. last round once. Change to No. 11 needle and rep. inc. round 4 times.
With No. 10 needles cast off.

To Make Up. Press lightly on wrong side with a warm iron over a damp cloth. Sew in sleeves, then join sleeves and side seams. Turn half of neck border to wrong side and sew down neatly. Press seams.

Lace-up sweater — in 5 sizes
Illustrated in colour on page 21

MATERIALS. 5 (5, 6, 7, 7) balls Wendy Tricel/Nylon Crepe double knitting in main shade and 3 (3, 3, 4, 5) balls in each of 2 contrasting shades (or any Tricel/Nylon double knitting yarn to give tension indicated below). One pair each No. 9 and No. 11 knitting needles (USA: sizes 5 and 2). One crochet hook International Standard Size 5.00.

MEASUREMENTS. To fit chest size 28/29 (31/32, 34/35, 37/38, 40/41) in.; length 19 (20½, 22, 23, 24) in.; length of sleeve seam 2½ (4, 4, 4, 5½) in.

TENSION. 6½ sts. to 1 in. and 1 patt. to 1½ in.

ABBREVIATIONS. See page 12; M., main shade; A, first contrasting shade; B., 2nd contrasting shade.

PATT.
1st to 4th rows: with M., work in st.st. beg. with a k. row.
5th to 8th rows: with A., work in st.st., beg. with a k. row.
9th row: with B., k. winding yarn 3 times round needle for each st. **10th row:** with B., p., letting extra 2 loops drop.

BACK
With No. 11 needles and M. cast on 92 (102, 112, 122, 132) sts. and work 20 rows in k.1, p.1 rib.
Change to No. 9 needles and patt. as given above. Work 7 (8, 9, 10, 11) patts. (of 10 rows each) straight.

Shape Raglan. Cont. in patt., cast off 4 sts. at beg. of next 2 rows. K.2 tog. at each end of next row. Work 3 rows straight. K.2 tog. at each end of every right-side row and at each end of every 10th patt. row until 34 (40, 46, 52, 58) sts. remain. K.2 tog. at each end of first 8 patt. rows and k.3 tog. at each end of every 9th and 10th patt. row until 28 (30, 32, 34, 36) sts. remain. Leave sts. on st. holder.

FRONT
Work as Back until 6 (7, 8, 9, 10) patts. have been completed.

Divide for Front Opening. Next 2 rows: patt. 46 (51, 56, 61, 66) sts.; turn and work back. Working on these sts. only, complete this patt.

Shape Raglan. Next 2 rows: cast off 4 sts., patt. to neck edge; turn and work back. K.2 tog. at beg. of next row. Work 3 rows in patt. K.2 tog. at beg. of every right-side row and at end of every 10th patt. row until 25 (29, 33, 37, 41) sts. remain, ending at neck edge.
Next row: patt. 9 (10, 11, 12, 13) sts. and place on st. holder, patt. to end of row. Now dec. at armhole edge as before and at neck edge on every right-side row, until 6 (7, 9, 10, 11) sts. remain. Now dec. at armhole edge only on every right-side row and on every 10th patt. row until all sts. are worked off. Rejoin yarn to other half of front opening and work to match first, reversing shapings.

SLEEVES (make 2 alike)
With No. 11 needles and M., cast on 64 (70, 76, 82, 88) sts. and work 10 rows in k.1, p.1 rib. Change to No. 9 needles and work 1 (2, 2, 2, 3) patts.

Shape Raglan. Cont. in patt. cast off 4 sts. at beg. of next 2 rows. K.2 tog. at each end of every right-side row and every 10th patt. row until 6 sts. remain. Work 2 more rows if necessary to match Back. Place sts. on safety pin.

TO COMPLETE
Front Opening. With No. 11 needles and M. and right-side facing, pick up and k. 25 (33, 38, 43, 48) sts. down left side of front opening from neck to base and 25 (33, 38, 43, 48) sts. up right side of opening: 50 (66, 76, 86, 96) sts. Beg. with a p. row, work 3 rows in st.st. P. 1 row. Beg. with a p. row, work 4 rows in st.st. Cast off loosely. Fold half of border to wrong side and hem.

Collar. Carefully join raglan seams. With right side facing, No. 11 needles and M., beg. at right front and pick up and k. 3 sts. from top of front opening border, k. 9 (10, 11, 12, 13) sts. from st. holder, pick up and k. 14 (16, 18, 20, 22) sts. round neck to shoulder, k. 6 sts. from shoulder safety pin, k. 28 (30, 32, 34, 36) sts. from neck st. holder, k. 6 sts. from other shoulder safety pin, pick up and k. 14 (16, 18, 20, 22) round neck to front st. holder, k. 9 (10, 11, 12, 13) sts. from holder, pick up and k. 3 sts. from front opening border: 92 (100, 108, 116, 124) sts.
Work 7 rows in k.1, p.1 rib. Cast off loosely in rib.

To Make Up. Join side and sleeve seams. With all 3 colours tog. and crochet hook, make a length of ch. to lace up front opening and tie at neck.

Teenage trouser suit
Illustrated in colour on page 28

MATERIALS. For jersey: 20 (21, 22) balls Wendy Tricel/Nylon double knitting (or any double knitting to give tension indicated below). One pair each No. 10 and No. 8 knitting needles (USA: sizes 3 and 6). **For trousers:** 18 (19, 20) balls Wendy Tricel/Nylon double knitting (or any double knitting to give tension indicated below). One pair each No. 10 and No. 8 knitting needles (USA: sizes 3 and 6). Waist length narrow elastic. **For tunic:** 14 (14, 15) balls Wendy Carolette knitting or 15 (16, 17) balls Wendy Courtellon double knitting (or any double knitting to give tension indicated below). One pair each No. 6 and No. 5 knitting needles (USA: sizes 8 and 9).

MEASUREMENTS. To fit bust size 32 (34, 36) in.; length of Jersey 22 (22½, 23) in.; length of Jersey sleeve seam 17 in.; Trousers inside leg measurement 27 (28, 29) in.; Trousers front waist to crutch measurement 10 (10½, 11) in.; length of Tunic 25 (26, 27) in. (all lengths adjustable).

TENSION. Jersey and Trousers: 5½ sts. and 7 rows to 1 in. over st.st. with No. 8 needles. **Tunic:** 3½ sts. and 7 rows to 1 in. over honeycomb patt. with No. 5 needles.

ABBREVIATIONS. See page 12.

JERSEY FRONT
With Tricel/Nylon and No. 10 needles cast on 96 (102, 108) sts. and work 2½ in. in k.1, p.1 rib. Change to No. 8 needles.
1st row: k.1 (3, 5), * k. twice into next st., k.3; rep. from * 8 times, k.22 (24, 26), ** k.3, k. twice into next st.; rep. from ** 8 times, k.1 (3, 5): 114 (120, 126) sts.
2nd row: * k.1, p.1; rep. from * 22 (23, 24) times, p.22 (24, 26), ** p.1, k.1; rep. from ** 22 (23, 24) times.
3rd row: * p.1, k.1; rep. from * 22 (23, 24) times, k.22 (24, 26), ** k.1, p.1; rep. from ** 22 (23, 24) times.
Keeping the centre panel of 22 (24, 26) sts. correct in st.st. and side panels in rib, cont. until work measures 14 in. from cast-on edge, ending with a wrong-side row (adjust length here if necessary).

Shape Armholes. Cont. in patt., cast off 5 sts. at beg. of next 2 rows. Dec. 1 st. at each end of next 5 (6, 7) rows and of foll. 3 alt. rows. ***
Work straight on rem. 88 (92, 96) sts. until armholes measure 5½ (6, 6½) in. ending with a wrong-side row.

Shape Front Neck. Next row: patt. 33 (34, 35); turn. Working on these sts. only, patt. another 11 rows, dec. 1 st. at neck edge on next and foll. alt. rows: 27 (28, 29) sts.

Shape Shoulder. Cast off 9 sts. at beg. of next and foll. alt. row, and 9 (10, 11) sts. at beg. of foll. alt. row.
Return to rem. sts. and slip first 22 (24, 26) sts. on to a st. holder then work on rem. sts. to match first side of neck, reversing shapings.

JERSEY BACK
Work as Front to ***. Work straight until Back matches Front to beg. of shoulder shaping.

Shape Shoulders. Cast off 9 sts. at beg. of next 4 rows and 9 (10, 11) sts. at beg. of foll. 2 rows. Leave rem. 34 (36, 38) sts. on st. holder.

JERSEY SLEEVES (make 2 alike)
With No. 10 needles cast on 42 (44, 46) sts. and work 3 in. in k.1, p.1 rib.
Next row (right side): * k. twice into next st.; rep. from * 9 (10, 11) times, rib 21, ** (k. twice into next st.); rep. from ** 8 (9, 10) times, k.2: 61 (65, 69) sts.
Change to No. 8 needles.
Next row: p.20 (22, 24), rib 21, p. 20 (22, 23).
Keeping the 21 sts. in centre correct in k.1, p.1 rib, and side panels in st.st., inc. 1 st. at each end of 3rd and every foll. 6th row until there are 85 (89, 93) sts. Work straight until Sleeve measures 17 in. (or required length) from cast-on edge, ending with a wrong-side row.

Shape Top. Cast off 5 sts. at beg. of next 2 rows and 2 sts. at beg. of foll. 22 (24, 26) rows. Cast off 4 sts. at beg. of next 2 rows. Cast off.

TO COMPLETE
Sew right shoulder seam.

Polo Neck With right side facing and No. 10 needles, beg. at left shoulder and pick up 17 sts. down side of front neck, 22 (24, 26) sts. from st. holder, 17 sts. up other side of front neck 34 (36, 38) sts. from st. holder at back neck: 90 (94, 98) sts.
Working in k.1, p.1 rib, work 1½ in. with No. 10 needles and 2½ in. with No. 8 needles. Cast off loosely in rib.

To Make Up. Press st.st. sections lightly on wrong side with a cool iron. Sew left shoulder seam, joining sides of polo neck as well. Sew side seams. Set in Sleeves and sew sleeve seams.
continued on page 22

Opposite page: *man's Aran sweater see page 12 for instructions.*

Above: *matching lace-up sweaters for all the family. Instructions start on page 18.*

TROUSERS FRONT

Right Leg. With Tricel/Nylon and No. 10 needles cast on 59 (61, 63) sts. and, beg. with a k. row, work 7 rows in st.st.
8th row (hemline): k.
Change to No. 8 needles.
1st row: k.
2nd row: p.29 (30, 31), keep y.f. and slip 1 purlwise, p.29 (30, 31).
Keeping the slipped st. correct in this fashion on all p. rows, cont. in st.st., dec. 1 st. at each end of 11th and every foll. 10th row until 47 (49, 51) sts. remain. Work straight until leg measures 22 (23, 24) in. from hemline, ending with a wrong-side row.
Cont. as before, inc. 1 st. at each end of next row.
For sizes 34 and 36 only. Inc. 1 st. at each end of foll. 10th row.
For all sizes: 49 (53, 55) sts. Work straight until Leg measures 27 (28, 29) in. (or required length) from hemline, ending with a wrong-side row. Leave these sts. on spare needle.

Left Leg. Work as right leg.
Join Legs and Shape Crutch. 1st row: k. across sts. for left leg, cast on 20 sts., k. across sts. for right leg.
2nd and alt. rows: p. keeping slipped sts. correct as before.
3rd row: k.48 (52, 54), k.2 tog. t.b.l., k.18, k.2 tog., k.48 (52, 54).
5th row: k.48 (52, 54), k.2 tog. t.b.l., k.16, k.2 tog., k.48 (52, 54).
Cont. to dec. 2 sts. in this way on every right-side row until 98 (106, 110) sts. remain. Work straight until Front measures 4½ (5, 5½) in. from joining legs, ending with a p. row. (adjust length here, if necessary).

Shape Waist. 1st row: k.2 tog., k.34 (38, 40), k.2 tog., k.22, k.2 tog. t.b.l., k.34 (38, 40), k.2 tog. t.b.l.
Keeping slipped sts. correct, patt. 3 rows.
5th row: k.2 tog., k.32 (36, 38), k.2 tog., k.22, k.2 tog. t.b.l., k.32 (36, 38), k.2 tog. t.b.l. Keeping slipped sts. always correct, and dec. 4 sts. in this way on every foll. 4th row, work until 62 (70, 74) sts. remain.
Patt. another 3 rows.
For sizes 34 and 36 only. Dec. 4 sts. as before on next row.
For all sizes. Waistband: 62 (66, 70) sts. Change to No. 10 needles and cont. in k.1, p.1 rib until Front measures 10 (10½, 11) in. (or required length) from joining legs. Cast off in rib.

TROUSERS BACK

Work as Front until Back is 1 row shorter than Front to beg. of waistband: 62 (66, 70) sts.

Shape Back. Next rows: keeping slipped sts. correct, patt. 54 (56, 58); turn; k.46; turn; patt. 40; turn; k.34; turn; patt. 28; turn; k.22; turn; patt. 16; turn; k.10; turn; patt. to end of row.
Change to No. 10 needles and work waistband to match Front.

TO COMPLETE

Press st.st. sections lightly on wrong side, using cool iron. Block hems and creases. Sew side seams and inner leg seams.

Turn up and catch st. hems in position. Press seams. Make a crochet casing inside waistband and thread with elastic.

TUNIC FRONT

With No. 6 needles and Carolette or Courtellon, cast on 60 (64, 68) sts. and k. 8 rows.
Change to No. 5 needles and patt.
1st row: k.1, * k. into st. below next st., k.1; rep. from * to last st., k.1.
2nd and 4th rows: k.
3rd row: k.2, * k. into st. below next st., k.1; rep. from * to end.
These last 4 rows form honeycomb patt. Cont. in patt. until work measures 16 (16½, 17) in. from cast-on edge, ending with a wrong-side row (adjust length here, if necessary).

Armhole Edgings. 1st row: k.2, patt. to last 2 sts., k.2.
2nd, 4th, 6th and 8th rows: k.
3rd row: k.3, patt. to last 3 sts., k.3.
5th row: k.4, patt. to last 4 sts., k.4.
7th row: k.5, patt. to last 5 sts., k.5.

Shape Armholes. 1st row: cast off 3, k.3 (including st. used in casting off), patt. to last 6 sts., k.6.
2nd row: cast off 3, k. to end.
3rd row: k.2, k.2 tog., patt. to last 4 sts., k.2 tog., k.2.
4th row: k.2, k.2 tog., k. to last 4 sts., k.2 tog., k.2.
Dec. 2 sts. in this way on next 1 (2, 3) rows and on foll. alt. row. keeping the 3 garter sts. correct at each end of needle, cont. straight in patt. on rem. 46 (48, 50) sts. until armholes measure 4½ (5, 5½) in. ending with a wrong-side row. ****

Neck Edging. 1st row: k.3, patt. 15 (16, 17), k.10, patt. 15 (16, 17), k.3.
2nd, 4th, 6th and 8th rows: k.
3rd row: k.3, patt. 14 (15, 16), k.12, patt. 14 (15, 16), k.3.
5th row: k.3, patt. 13 (14, 15), k.14, patt. 13 (14, 15), k.3.
7th row: k.3, patt. 12 (13, 14), k.16, patt. 12 (13, 14), k.3.

Shape Neck. 1st row: k.3, patt. 11 (12, 13), k.2 tog., k.2, cast off 10, k.2 (including st. used in casting off), k.2 tog., patt. 11 (12, 13), k.3.
Work on last set of sts. only.
Next row: k.
Next row: k.2, k.2 tog., patt. to last 3 sts., k.3: 16 (17, 18) sts.
Rep. these last 2 rows 3 times more: 13 (14, 15) sts. Keeping the 3 garter sts. at each end always correct, patt. another 6 rows.
Cast off 3 sts. at beg. of next row, 7 (8, 9) sts. at beg. of next alt. row. and 3 sts. at beg. of foll. alt. row.
Return to rem. sts. and work to match first side of neck, reversing shapings.

TUNIC BACK

Work as Front to ****. Work straight until Back is 10 rows shorter than Front to beg. of shoulder casting-off.

Neck Edging. 1st row: k.3, patt. 10 (11, 12), k.20, patt. 10 (11, 12), k.3.
2nd, 4th, 6th and 8th rows: k.
3rd row: k.3, patt. 9 (10, 11), k.22, patt. 9 (10, 11), k.3.
5th row: k.3, patt. 8 (9, 10), k.24, patt. 8 (9, 10), k.3.
7th row: k.3, patt. 7 (8, 9), k.26, patt. 7 (8, 9), k.3.

Shape Neck. 1st row: k.3, patt. 7 (8, 9), k.3 cast off 20, k.3 (including st. used in casting off), patt. 7 (8, 9), k.3.
Work on last set of sts. only. Cont. in patt., cast off 3 sts. at beg. of next row, 7 (8, 9) sts. at beg. of next alt. row, and 3 sts. at beg. of foll. alt. row.
Return to rem. sts. and work to match first side of neck, reversing shapings.

TO COMPLETE

Do not press. Sew shoulder seams and side seams.

Little girl's three-piece
Illustrated in colour on page 25

MATERIALS. For cape: 6 (7, 7) balls (1¾ oz.) Mahony's Blarney Heatherspun Quicker Knitting. One pair No. 7 knitting needles. One cable needle. 4 buttons ⅝ in. in diameter. **For pinafore dress:** 4 (4, 5) balls (1¾ oz.) Mahony's Blarney Heatherspun Quicker Knitting. One pair each No. 7 and No. 8 knitting needles. One cable needle. **For jersey:** 4 (5, 5) balls (1¾ oz.) Mahony's Blarney Berella Baby Quickerknit. One pair each No. 8 and No. 10 knitting needles. One cable needle. 6 snap fasteners.

MEASUREMENTS. To fit chest size 22 (23, 24) in.; length of Cape from shoulder to lower edge 15½ (16¾, 18)in.; length of Pinafore Dress 14 (15¼, 16½) in.; length of Jersey 12½ (13½, 14½) in.; length of Jersey sleeve seam 7½ (8¼, 9) in.

TENSION. Cape and pinafore dress: 10 sts. and 13 rows to 2 in. over reversed st.st. Jersey: 13 sts. and 17 rows to 2 in. over reversed st.st.

ABBREVIATIONS. See page 12; m.1, make 1: pick up loop lying between last and next st. and k. it t.b.l.; c.2 b., cable 2 back: slip next st. on to cable needle and leave at back of work, k.1 t.b.l., then p.1 from cable needle; c.2 f., cable 2 front: slip next st. on to cable needle and leave at front of work, p.1, then k.1 t.b.l. from cable needle.

PATT. (11 sts.)
1st row (right side): * k.1 t.b.l., p.3, k.3 t.b.l., p.3, k.1 t.b.l. *
2nd row: * p.1, k.3, p.3, k.3, p.1. *
3rd row: * k.1 t.b.l., p.2, c.2 b., k.1 t.b.l., c.2 f., p.2, k.1 t.b.l. *
4th row: * p.1, k.2, (p.1, k.1) twice, p.1, k.2, p.1. *
5th row: * k.1 t.b.l., p.1, c.2 b., p.1, k.1 t.b.l., c.2 f., p.1, k.1 t.b.l. *
6th row: * p.1, k.1, (p.1, k.2) twice, p.1, k.1, p.1. *
7th row: k.1 t.b.l., c.2 b., p.2, k.1 t.b.l., p.2, c.2 f., k.1 t.b.l. *
8th row: * p.1, (k.4, p.1) twice. *

CAPE BACK
With No. 7 needles, cast on 100 (107, 114) sts. P. 6 rows. Now beg. patt. panels.
1st row: p.18 (21, 24), work from * to * of first row of patt., p.2, work from * to *, p.16 (17, 18), work from * to *, p.2, work from * to *, p.18 (21, 24).
2nd row: k.18 (21, 24), work from * to * of 2nd row of patt., k.2, work from * to *, k.16 (17, 18), work from * to *, k.2, work from * to *, k.18 (21, 24).
3rd row: p.18 (21, 24), work from * to * of 3rd row of patt., p.2, work from * to *, p.16 (17, 18), work from * to *, p.2, work from * to *, p.18 (21, 24).
4th row: k.18 (21, 24), work from * to * of 4th row of patt.,

k.2, work from * to *, k.15 (17, 18), work from * to *, k.2, work from * to *, k.18 (21, 24).
5th row: p.18 (21, 24), work from * to * of 5th row of patt., p.2, work from * to *, p.16 (17, 18), work from * to *, p.2, work from * to *, p.18 (21, 24).
6th row: k.18 (21, 24), work from * to * of 6th row of patt., k.2, work from * to *, k.16 (17, 18), work from * to *, k.2, work from * to *, k.18 (21, 24).
7th row: p.18 (21, 24), work from * to * of 7th row of patt., p.2, work from * to *, p.16 (17, 18), work from * to *, p.2, work from * to *, p.18 (21, 24).
8th row: k.18 (21, 24), work from * to * of 8th row of patt., k.2, work from * to *, k.16 (17, 18), work from * to *, k.2, work from * to *, k.18 (21, 24).
Cont. in this way with patt. panels and reversed st.st.
Keeping continuity of panels, dec. 1 st. at each end of next row and every foll. first patt. row until 82 (87, 92) sts. remain. Cont. straight until 10 (11, 12) patts. have been completed.
Next row: p.2 tog., p.18 (20, 22), p.2 tog., p.38 (39, 40), p.2 tog., p.18 (20, 22), p.2 tog.: 78 (83, 88) sts.
Cont. in reversed st.st. only.
Dec. 1 st. at each end of foll. alt. rows twice: 74 (79, 84) sts. Work 1 row. Dec. 1 st. at each end of next 4 rows: 66 (71, 76) sts.

Shape Shoulders. Cast off 6 (6, 7) sts. at beg. of next 6 rows. Cast off 6 (8, 9) sts. at beg. of foll. 2 rows: 18 (19, 20) sts. Cast off.

CAPE LEFT FRONT
With No. 7 needles cast on 50 (53, 56) sts. P.6 rows. Now beg. patt. panels.
1st row: p.18 (21, 24), work from * to * of first row of patt., p.2, work from * to *, p.8.
2nd row: k.8, work from * to * of 2nd row of patt., k.2, work from * to *, k.18 (21, 24).
Now cont. in patt. as set until 1 patt. has been completed. Keeping continuity of panels, dec. 1 st. at beg. (side edge) of next row and every foll. first patt. row until 48 (50, 52) sts. remain. Cont. straight until 3 (4, 5) patts. have been completed.

Slot Opening. Next row: p.2 tog., p.14 (16, 18), work from * to * of first row of patt., p. twice into next st.; turn. Cont. on these 28 (30, 32) sts. only.
Next row: k.2, p.1, k.3, p.3, k.3, p.1, k.15 (17, 19).
Cont. in patt., still dec. 1 st. at side edge on every first patt. row until 25 (27, 29) sts. remain. Cont. straight until the 7th row of the 7th (8th, 9th) patt. has been worked. Break yarn. With right side facing rejoin yarn to inner edge of rem. 20 sts. Cont. straight until the 7th row of the 7th (8th, 9th) patt. has been worked.
Next row: k.8, p.1, (k.4, p.1) twice, k. next st. tog. with first st. of other side, k.1, p.1, (k.4, p.1) twice, k.12 (14, 16): 44 (46, 48) sts. Dec. 1 st. at side edge on next row and every foll. first patt. row until 41 (43, 45) sts. remain. Cont. straight until 10 (11, 12) patts. have been completed.
Next row: p.2 tog., p.18 (20, 22), p.2 tog., p.19: 39 (41, 43) sts.
Cont. in reversed st.st. only. Dec. 1 st. at side edge on foll. alt. rows twice: 37 (39, 41) sts., ending at front edge.

Shape Neck and Shoulders. Next row: cast off 5 sts., k. to end: 32 (34, 36) sts. Dec. 1 st. at each end of next 4 rows: 24 (26, 28) sts. Cast off 6 (6, 7) sts. at beg. of next row and every foll. alt. row until 6 (8, 7) sts. remain. Work 1 row. Cast off.

CAPE RIGHT FRONT
With No. 7 needles, cast on 50 (53, 56)sts. P. 6 rows. Beg. patt. panels.
1st row: p.8, work from * to * of first row of patt., p.2, work from * to *, p.18 (21, 24).
2nd row: k.18 (21, 24), work from * to * of 2nd row of patt., k.2, work from * to *, k.8.

23

Cont. in patt. as set. Work straight until 1 patt. has been completed. Keeping continuity of panels, dec. 1 st. at end (side edge) next row and every foll. first patt. row until 48 (50, 52) sts. remain. Cont. straight until 3 (4, 5) patts. have been completed.

Slot Opening. Next row: p.8, work from * to * of first row of patt., p.1; turn.

Cont. straight on these 20 sts. until the 7th row of the 7th (8th, 9th) patt. has been worked. Break yarn.

With right side facing, rejoin yarn to inner edge of rem. 28 (30, 32) sts., p. twice into first st., work from * to * of first patt. row, p.14 (16, 18), p.2 tog.: 28 (30, 32) sts.

Next row: k.15 (17, 19), p.1, k.3, p.3, k.3, p.1, k.2.

Cont. in patt., still dec. 1 st. at side edge on every foll. first patt. row until 25 (27, 29) sts. remain. Cont. straight until the 7th row of the 7th (8th, 9th) patt. has been completed.

Next row: k.12 (14, 16), p.1, (k.4, p.1) twice, k.1, k. next st. tog. with first st. of other side, p.1, (k.4, p.1) twice, k.8: 44 (46, 48) sts. Dec. 1 st. at side edge on next row and every foll. first patt. row until 41 (43, 45) sts. remain. Cont. straight until 10 (11, 12) patts. have been worked.

Next row: p.19, p.2 tog., p.18 (20, 22), p.2 tog.: 39 (41, 43) sts.

Cont. in reversed st.st. only. Dec. 1 st. at side edge on foll. alt. rows twice: 37 (39, 41) sts. ending at side edge.

Shape Neck and Shoulders. Next row: k.32 (34, 36), cast off rem. 5 sts. and break yarn. Rejoin yarn to last st. Dec. 1 st. at each end of next 4 rows: 24 (26, 28) sts. Work 1 row. Cast off 6 (6, 7) sts. at beg. of next row and every foll. alt. row until 6 (8, 7) sts. remain. Work 1 row. Cast off.

COLLAR

With No. 7 needles, cast on 55 (58, 61) sts.

1st row: k.4, p. to last 4 sts., k.4.

2nd row: k.

** Rep. first and 2nd rows once, then first row again.

Opposite: *Fair Isle jerseys and caps (see page 15).* **Above and right:** *pink and white three-piece for a toddler (see page 23).*

Inc. row: k.4, m.1, k. to last 4 sts., m.1, k.4. **
Rep. last 4 rows from ** to ** twice more. K. 5 rows. Cast off.

TO COMPLETE
Front Borders. With right side of Right Front facing and with No. 7 needles, pick up and k.68 (74, 80) sts. along front edge. k. 1 (3, 3) rows.
Buttonhole row: k.35 (38, 41), * y.f., k.2 tog. t.bl., k.8 (9, 10); rep. from * ending last rep. with k.1.
K. 2 (2, 4) rows. Cast off.
Work along Left Front to match but omit buttonholes.

Slot Opening Borders. With right side of Right Front facing and with No. 7 needles, pick up and k. 25 sts. along edge of opening nearer front edge. K. 4 rows. Cast off.
With right side facing and with No. 7 needles, pick up and k. 25 sts. along edge of opening nearest side edge. Cast off.
Work Left Front to match.

To Make Up. Press work on the wrong side using a hot iron over a damp cloth. Sew underwrap of each slot opening into position. Press. Sew up shaped side and shoulder seams. Press seams. Sew Collar round neck edge. Press seam. Sew buttons on to Left Front to correspond with buttonholes.

PINAFORE DRESS
BACK
With No. 7 needles, cast on 74 (81, 88) sts. P. 4 rows. Now beg. patt. panels.
1st row: p.18 (21, 24), work from * to * of first row of patt., p.16 (17, 18), work from * to *, p. 18 (21, 24).
2nd row: k.18 (21, 24), work from * to * of 2nd row of patt., k.16 (17, 18), work from * to *, k.18 (21, 24).
3rd row: p.18 (21, 24), work from * to * of 3rd row of patt., p.16 (17, 18), work from * to *, p.18 (21, 24).
Now cont. as set with patt. panels and reversed st.st. Cont. straight until 1 completes patt. has been worked.
Keeping continuity of panels, dec. 1 st. at each end of next row and every foll. first patt. row until 62 (67, 72) sts. remain.
Cont. straight until the 8th (6th, 4th) row of the 7th (8th, 9th) patt. has been worked.

Shape Armholes. Cast off 5 (6, 7) sts. at beg. of next 2 rows: 52 (55, 58) sts. Dec. 1 st. at each end of next 5 rows: 42 (45, 48) sts.
Work 1 (3, 5) rows, thus completing the 8th (9th, 10th) patt.
***
Cont. straight until the 10th (11th, 12th) patt. has been completed.

Shape Neck. **** Next row:** patt. 13 (14, 15), cast off next 16 (17, 18) sts., patt. to end. Cont. on last set of 13 (14, 15) sts. only. Dec. 1 st. at neck edge on next 3 rows: 10 (11, 12) sts. Cont. straight until the 11th (12th, 13th) patt. has been completed. Cast off.
With wrong side facing rejoin yarn to inner edge of rem. 13 (14, 15) sts. Work as for first side.

FRONT
Work as Back to ***: 42 (45, 48) sts.

Shape Front Neck. Work as Back from **** to end.

TO COMPLETE
Neck Borders. With right side of Front facing and with No. 7 needles, pick up and k. 56 (57, 58) sts. round neck edge. K. 1 row. Change to No. 8 needles, k. 1 row. Cast off.
With right side of Back facing and with No. 7 needles, pick up and k.32 (33, 34) sts. along neck edge. Work as for Front Neck.

Armhole Borders. Press work on the wrong side using a hot iron over a damp cloth. Sew up shoulder seams. Press seams.

With right side of work facing and with No. 7 needles, pick up and k.61 (64, 67) sts. round one armhole edge. Work as for neck borders.
Work round other armhole in same way.
Sew up side seams. Press seams.

Armhole Borders. Press work on the wrong side using a hot iron over a damp cloth. Sew up shoulder seams. Press seams.
With right side of work facing and with No. 7 needles, pick up and k.61 (65, 67) sts. round one armhole edge. Work as for neck borders.
Work round other armhole in same way.
Sew up side seams. Press seams.

JERSEY BACK
With No. 10 needles cast on 81 (87, 93) sts.
1st row (right side): p.1, * k.1, p.1; rep. from * to end.
2nd row: k.1, * p.1, k.1; rep. from * to end.
Rep. first and 2nd rows 5 times more, inc. 1 st. at each end of last row: 83 (89, 95) sts.
Change to No. 8 needles and beg. patt. panel.
1st row: p.36 (39, 42), work from * to * of first row of patt., p. 36 (39, 42).
2nd row: k.36 (39, 42), work from * to * of 2nd row of patt., p.36 (39, 42).
3rd row: p.36 (39, 42), work from * to * of 3rd row of patt., p. 36 (39, 42).
Cont. as set, with side panels of reversed st.st. and centre panel of patt. Cont. straight until 7 (8, 8) complete patts. have been worked. Work 2 (0, 6) rows of next patt.

Shape Armholes. Cast off 3 sts. at beg. of next 2 rows: 77 (83, 89) sts. Dec. 1 st. at each end of next 4 rows. Dec. 1 st. at each end of foll. alt. rows 2 (3, 4) times: 65 (69, 73) sts.
*****.
Cont. straight until 11 (12, 13) complete patts. have been worked. Work 2 rows of next patt.

Shape Shoulders. Cast off 7 sts. at beg. of next 4 rows. Cast off 6 (7, 8) sts. at beg. of foll. 2 rows: 25 (27, 29) sts. Cast off.

JERSEY FRONT
Work as Back to *****: 65 (69, 73) sts. Cont. straight until 10 (11, 12) complete patts. have been worked.

Shape Neck. Next row: p. 26 (27, 28), cast off next 13 (15, 17) sts., p. to end.
Cont. on last set of 26 (27, 28) sts. only. Dec. 1 st. at neck edge on next 4 rows. Dec. 1 st. at neck edge on foll. alt. rows twice: 20 (21, 22) sts. Work 2 rows ending at armhole edge.

Shape Shoulder. Cast off 7 sts. at beg. of next row and foll. alt. row: 6 (7, 8) sts. Work 1 row. Cast off.
With wrong side facing rejoin yarn to inner edge of rem. 26 (27, 28) sts. Work as for first side but work only 1 row (instead of 2 rows) before shaping shoulder.

SLEEVES (make 2 alike)
With No. 10 needles, cast on 37 (39, 41) sts.
Work 12 rows in rib as given for Back, inc. 1 st. at each end of last row: 39 (41, 43) sts.
Change to No. 8 needles and beg. patt. panel.
1st row: p.14 (15, 16), work from * to * of first row of patt., p.14 (15, 16).
2nd row: k.14 (15, 16), work from * to * of 2nd row of patt., k.14 (15, 16).
3rd row: p.14 (15, 16), work from * to * of 3rd row of patt., p.14 (15, 16).
Cont. as set in patt. and reversed st.st. Cont. straight until 1 patt. has been worked. Working inc. sts. into reversed st.st., inc. 1 st. at each end of next row and every foll. first patt. row until there are 51 (53, 55) sts.

Cont. straight until Sleeve measures 7½ (8¼, 9) in. from cast-on edge, ending with a wrong-side row.

Shape Top. Cast off 3 sts. at beg. of next 2 rows: 45 (47, 49) sts. Dec. 1 st. at each end of next row and every foll. alt. row until 37 sts. remain. Work 1 row. Dec. 1 st. at each end of next 6 rows: 25 sts. Cast off 3 sts. at beg. of next 4 rows: 13 sts. Cast off.

TO COMPLETE

Neck Ribbing. With right side of Front facing and with No. 10 needles, pick up and k.39 (41, 43) sts. round neck edge. Work 5 rows in rib as given for Back, beg. with a 2nd row. Cast off in rib.
With right side of Back facing and with No. 10 needles, pick up and k.25 (27, 29) sts. along back neck edge. Work as for front neck ribbing.

Shoulder Borders. Press work on the wrong side using a warm iron over a dry cloth, avoiding all ribbing. Sew up shoulder seams for the length of 10 sts. from armhole edges. Press seams.
With right side facing and with No. 8 needles pick up and k.31 sts. round one shoulder opening. K. 2 rows. Cast off knitwise. Work round other shoulder opening in same way. Sew sleeves into armholes. Press seams. Sew up side and sleeve seams. Press seams. Lap front shoulders over back shoulders. Sew 3 snap fasteners on to each shoulder opening.

Evening suit

Illustrated in colour on page 29

MATERIALS. For waistcoat: 6 (7, 7, 8) oz. Twilley's Cortina Super Crochet Wool and 7 (7, 8, 9) oz. Twilley's Goldfingering. One pair each No. 10 and No. 12 Knitting needles (USA: sizes 3 and 1). **For skirt:** 8 (9, 10, 11) oz. Twilley's Cortina Super Crochet and 8 (9, 10, 11) oz. Twilley's Goldfingering. One pair each No. 10 and No. 12 knitting needles (USA: sizes 3 and 1). ¾ yard elastic 1 in. wide.

MEASUREMENTS. to fit bust size 32 (34, 36, 38) in. and hip size 34 (36, 38, 40) in.; length of Waistcoat 27 (27, 28, 28) in.; length of Skirt 30 in. (adjustable).

TENSION. 8 sts. and 11 rows to 1 in. with Goldfingering; 7 sts. and 10 rows to 1 in. with Cortina.

ABBREVIATIONS. See page 12; G., Goldfingering; C., Cortina.

WAISTCOAT BACK

With No. 12 needles and G. cast on 136 (144, 152, 160) sts. Work 6 rows st.st., beg. with a p. row. K. 1 row for hemline. Now work in patt.
** With No. 12 needles and G. work 6 rows in st.st. beg. with a k. row.
With C. k. 1 row.
Change to No. 10 needles. With C. work 7 rows in reversed st.st., beg. with a k. row.
Change to No. 12 needles. With G. work 6 rows in st.st., beg. with a k. row.
With C. k. 1 row.
Change to No. 10 needles. With C. work 3 rows in reversed st.st. beg. with a k. row. **
These 24 rows from ** to ** form patt. Cont. straight in patt. until work measures 19 (19, 19½, 19½) in. from hemline.

Shape Armholes. Keeping patt. correct, cast off 10 (11, 12, 13) sts. at beg. of next 2 rows then dec. 1 st. at each end of next 10 rows: 96 (102, 108, 114) sts. Cont. straight in patt. until work measures 27 (27, 28, 28) in. from hemline.

Shape Shoulders. Cast off 8 (9, 10, 11) sts. at beg. of next 6 rows. Cast off.

RIGHT FRONT

With No. 12 needles and G. cast on 60 (64, 68, 72) sts. Work as Back until Front measures 19 (19, 19½, 19½) in. from hemline, ending with a right-side row.

Shape Armhole. Cast off 10 (11, 12, 13) sts. at beg. of next row then dec. 1 st. at armhole edge on next 10 rows: 40 (43, 46, 49) sts. Cont. straight in patt. until work measures 25 (25, 26, 26) in. from hemline, ending with a wrong-side row.

Shape Neck. Cast off 8 sts. at beg. of next row then dec. 1 st. at neck edge on next 8 rows: 24 (27, 30, 33) sts. Cont. straight until work measures 27 (27, 28, 28) in. from hemline ending at armhole edge.

Shape Shoulder. Cast off 8 (9, 10, 11) sts. at beg. of next and foll. 2 alt. rows.

LEFT FRONT

Work as Right Front reversing all shapings.

TO COMPLETE

Press lightly. Join shoulder and side seams. Fold hem at lower edge to wrong side and sew down. Press seams.

SKIRT

BACK AND FRONT (make 2 pieces alike)
With No. 12 needles and G. cast on 104 (112, 120, 128) sts. Work 24 rows in patt. as for Waistcoat Back.
Next row: with No. 12 needles and G. k.8, * k. twice into next st., k.7; rep. from * to end.
Work 47 rows straight in patt.
Next row: with No. 12 needles and G. k.8, * k. twice into next st., k.8; rep. from * to end.
Work 47 rows in patt.
Next row: with No. 12 needles and G. k.8, * k. twice into next st., k.9; rep. from * to end. Inc. in this way on first patt. row of every alt. patt. until the 6th inc. row has been completed: 176 (190, 204, 218) sts.
Cont. straight in patt. until work measures 30 in. from beg., ending with 6 rows in G. (adjust length here if required).
With No. 12 needles and G. p. 1 row for hemline, then work 6 rows in st.st., beg. with a p. row. Cast off loosely purlwise.

TO COMPLETE

Press lightly. Join side seams. Fold hem at lower edge to wrong side and sew down. Cut elastic to fit waist and join. Place inside waist and work herringbone st. over it to hold it in position. Press seams.

Opposite: *teenager's three-piece trouser suit –
see page 19 for instructions.*

Above: *elegant evening suit in plain and glitter
yarns. Instructions start on page 27.*

Chapter two
CROCHET

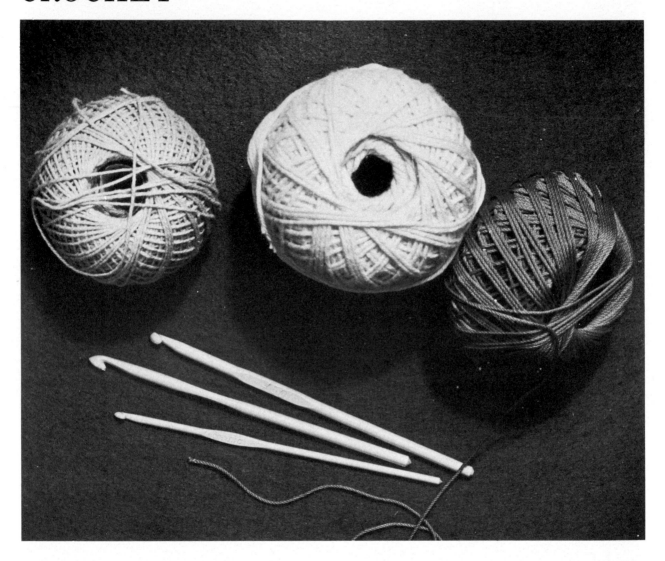

Of all forms of needlecraft, crochet is one of the simplest: little in the way of equipment is required, the craft is easy and quick to learn as it is based on variations of a single stitch, and because you work with only one stitch at a time – not a row of stitches as in knitting – it is easy to carry your work around with you. Crochet work usually grows faster than knitting too. Once crochet was used mainly for lacy patterns, for trimmings and edgings. Now however, worked in a variety of yarns and stitch patterns, it is possible to make all sorts of exciting fashion garments.

EQUIPMENT

A crochet hook and a ball of yarn are all you need to begin to crochet, but you will find it useful also to have a tape measure for measuring your work as you go along, pins for pinning the finished work out to the correct size, an iron, ironing board and cloth for pressing the completed item and a sewing needle for making it up. Hooks are available in many sizes from very thin to quite thick. The thin ones are used with fine cotton yarn and the thick with heavy wools or synthetics. In the system of sizing called International Standard Sizing the higher the size number the thicker the hook (see opposite). Hooks are available in steel, aluminium or plastic; steel hooks are generally used for work with fine cotton yarns and either aluminium or plastic for work with other yarns. Although a pattern normally recommends a particular size of hook, it is important not necessarily to use this hook size, but to use the one with which you can achieve the correct tension as quoted in the pattern (see page 35).

GUIDE TO CROCHET HOOK SIZES

International Standard Size	Old UK Sizes Wool	Old UK Sizes Cotton	American Sizes Wool	American Sizes Cotton
7.00	2	–	K	
–	3	–	–	
6.00	4	–	–	
5.50	5	–	–	
5.00	6	–	J	
4.50	7	–	I	
4.00	8	–	H	
3.50	9	–	G	
3.00	10	3/0	F	2/0
–	11	2/0	E	0
2.50	12	0	D	1
–	13	1	C	2
–	–	–	–	3
2.00	14	1½	B	4
–	–	2	A	5
1.75	15	2½	–	6
–	–	3	–	6
1.50	16	3½	–	7
–	–	4	–	8
1.25	–	4½	–	9
–	–	5	–	10
1.00	–	5½	–	11
–	–	6	–	12
0.75	–	6½	–	13
0.60	–	7	–	14
–	–	7½	–	–

Yarns

Traditionally very fine thread – usually cotton – is used for crochet trimmings and laces, but now so many other items can be successfully crocheted, wool and synthetic yarns and mixtures can all be used as well. In fact the extensive range of yarn types, thicknesses and colours available for knitting can be used with equal success for crochet work. The choice of yarn is, of course, dependent on the article being made, and the amount of wear it will have to withstand.

HOLDING YOUR HOOK

Pass the yarn round the little finger of the left hand, under the middle two fingers then over the first finger. The hook is held in the right hand; it rests between thumb and first finger rather like holding a pencil, with the second finger on the tip of the hook. Initially the loose end of the yarn is held tight between thumb and first finger of the left hand. When work begins, the work is held by the left hand between thumb and first finger. The left hand also controls the yarn from the main ball while the right hand moves the hook.

Left-handed workers will work in reverse, holding the hook in the left hand and controlling yarn with the right hand. The easiest way for left-handed workers to follow diagrams intended for right-hand workers is to place a pocket mirror at right angles to the diagrams, and follow the mirror-reflected diagrams.

STITCHES
Chain

This is the foundation of all crochet work, and for this reason it is often called 'foundation chain', though this stitch is also used at other times in the course of a pattern.

When making foundation chain you have to start with a slip loop. Undo a short length of yarn from the ball. Hold yarn between thumb and first finger of left hand and take yarn from ball in right hand; cross main yarn from ball over short length to make a loop then hold this loop firmly in the left hand. Take crochet hook in right hand and insert it into loop and with it pull through the main yarn so a loop forms on the hook. Pull short length of yarn to tighten loop on hook.

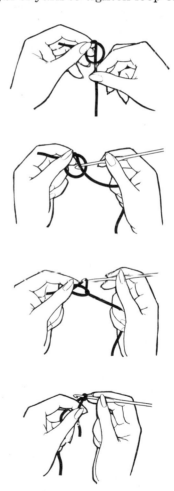

You are now ready to work your commencing chain – chain used as part of a pattern are worked in a similar way. Holding the short end of the yarn and the bottom of the slip loop between your left thumb and first finger, and yarn and hook in correct positions, take the hook under

31

A smart trouser suit that is quick and easy to crochet – see page 36 for instructions.

the yarn on the left-hand first finger and pull the yarn and hook through the loop on the hook.

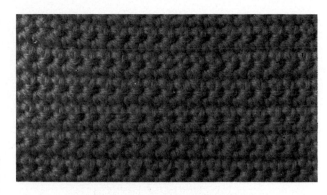

You have now worked one chain. The action of taking the hook under the yarn is called 'yarn over hook'. Continue making chain in this way until you have the number you want. Move your first finger and thumb of left hand up the chain as you work so you are always holding the chain just made.

yarn over the hook again and draw through the two loops on the hook. Continue in this way along row.

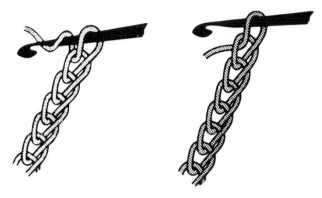

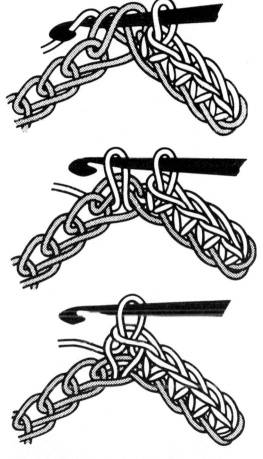

Slip stitch or single crochet

This stitch adds no height to the work, so can be used to take yarn across the work to another point, for joining or for making an edge firm. Work from right to left across foundation chain. Insert hook under top two loops of next chain (or stitch when working into a row of stitches instead of the foundation chain), yarn over hook and pull yarn through the chain stitch and through the loop on the hook. Insert hook into next stitch and repeat; continue in this way along row.

Double crochet

Insert hook into chain or stitch through top two loops, yarn over hook and draw through the stitch. This makes two loops on the hook. Take

Double crochet worked to give a dense, interlocked fabric.

Half treble

Take yarn over hook then insert hook into next stitch. Yarn over hook again and pull a loop through the stitch – three loops on the hook. Pass yarn over hook again and draw yarn through all three loops. Work along row in this way.

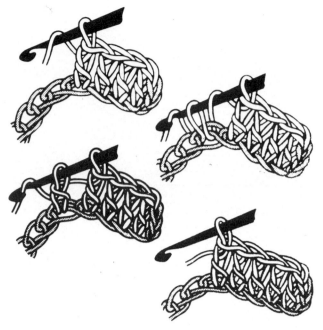

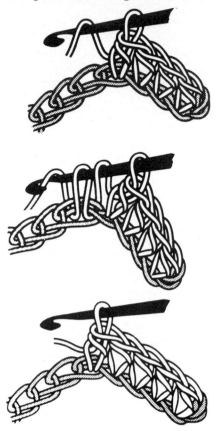

Treble

Pass yarn over hook then insert hook into next stitch. Yarn over hook and draw through stitch – three loops on hook. Yarn over hook again and draw through the first two loops on the hook. Yarn over hook once more and draw through remaining two loops on hook. Continue in this way along row.

Double treble

Take yarn over hook twice, then insert hook into next stitch. Yarn over hook and draw a loop through the stitch – four loops on hook. Yarn over hook and draw through two loops, yarn over hook again and draw through a further two loops, yarn over hook once more and draw through last two loops. Continue in this way all along row.

Triple treble

Yarn over hook three times, insert hook into next stitch, yarn over hook and draw through a loop – five loops on the hook. Yarn over hook and draw through two loops on the hook, yarn over hook and draw through two more loops on hook, yarn over hook and draw through two more loops, yarn over hook and draw through last two loops. Continue in this way along row.

TURNING CHAIN

As crochet stitches are worked from the top down, when crocheting in rows a new row cannot start until the yarn has been taken up to the correct height to begin the new row. To do this, a number of chain stitches are worked and these count as the first stitch in the row. At the end of the following row, the last stitch is worked into the top of these 'turning chain' as they are called. The number of turning chain worked will depend on the depth of the stitch being used in the pattern. Most patterns will tell you how many chain to work, but as a general guide work two chain for a double crochet stitch or a half treble, three chain for a treble stitch, four chain for a double treble, and five chain for a triple treble.

INCREASING

The most usual method of increasing is to work two stitches into the same stitch of the previous row – or more if this is required. If extra stitches are required at the edge of the work, a length of chain can be made at the end of a row and these chain stitches worked into on the following row.

DECREASING

If several stitches are to be decreased at the edge of the work, this can be done in the following way: at the beginning of a row work slip stitches over the number of stitches you want decreased; at the end of a row stop working the required number of stitches before the end, turn and work next row.

In some patterns, decreases can be made merely by missing a stitch, but a more successful method is to work two stitches together.

Work the first stitch in the usual way but leave the last loop of it on the hook (so there are two loops on hook); move on to next stitch and work this but leave the last loop on the hook. Take yarn over hook and draw through the last three loops on the hook.

FASTENING OFF

When your piece of work is complete – or if you are changing the colour of your yarn, or for some other reason want to fasten off – cut the yarn a few inches from the work. Pull this end through the last loop on the hook and draw tightly. Darn this loose end in later.

TENSION

The tension is the number of stitches and rows which measure one square inch for a particular pattern. In order to make an item of the correct finished size, you must work to the tension measurement given – e.g. if a pattern gives a tension of 6 rows and 8 stitches to the square inch, then you must make sure that your work achieves exactly this measurement, being neither slacker nor tighter. Before starting work on any pattern, check your tension by working a 3 or 4-in. square in the stitch pattern, yarn and hook size given in the pattern. Press the square then mark off on it with pins a 2-in. square. Count the number of stitches and rows contained in this square and compare them with the tension measurement given in the pattern. If there are more than those given, work another square with a hook a size larger; if there are fewer try again with a hook a size smaller.

Continue to make tension checks until you achieve exactly the right measurement. Do not ever start work on a pattern until you have found the right hook to give you the correct tension measurement.

JOINING YARN

When your ball of yarn is running out, take the new ball and lay the end of it on top of your work. Crochet over this with the last of the old ball for a few stitches, then lay the end of the old ball over the top of the work and crochet over it with the new ball.

SIMPLE PATTERNS

Picots

These are used as a decorative edging for many items.

There is more than one type of picot but the simplest method is to work to the required position of the picot, then make four chain and work a slip stitch into the fourth chain from hook: a picot made. Continue working to required position for next picot and repeat picot.

Shells

These are also usually worked in trebles. Working into foundation chain, miss two chain, work one double crochet into the next chain, miss two chain, work five trebles into next chain, and continue in this way to end of row. On next row, work the double crochet stitches into the centre trebles of the shells, and work the shells into the double crochet stitches.

Clusters or groups

These are usually worked in trebles. If you are working into foundation chain, leaving last loop of each on hook, work three trebles into one chain (four loops on hook), yarn over hook and

35

Example of a treble cluster pattern.

draw through all loops on hook, one chain, miss one chain, work another cluster, and continue along row in this way. On the next row work the clusters into the chain spaces of previous row.

Crab stitch

This is double crochet worked from left to right. It makes a good edging, particularly for a jacket or similar item.

ABBREVIATIONS

The following are the abbreviations normally used in crochet patterns.

alt.	alternate
beg.	beginning
blk(s).	block(s)
ch.	chain
cl.	cluster
cont.	continue
d.c.	double crochet
dec.	decreas(e) (ed) (ing)
d.tr.	double treble
foll.	following
gr(s).	group(s)
h.tr.	half treble
in.	inch(es)
inc.	increas(e) (ed) (ing)
p.	picot
patt.	pattern
rep.	repeat
sh.	shell
sp(s).	space(s)

s.s.	slip stitch
st(s).	stitch(es)
tog.	together
tr.	treble
tr.tr.	triple treble
y.o.h.	yarn over hook

Pattern sizes. If a pattern gives a range of different sizes, then normally instructions are given in size order, with the different instructions relating to larger sizes in brackets. Where only one set of figures occurs this refers to all sizes.

THE PATTERNS

Red trouser suit
Illustrated in colour on page 32

MATERIALS. For top: 17 (18, 19) 20-gram balls Patons Brilliante 4 ply (or any 4 ply to give tension as indicated below); 5 medium buttons. **For trousers:** 23 (24, 25) 20-gram balls Patons Brilliante 4 ply (or any 4 ply to give tension as indicated below); waist length of elastic. **For both:** crochet hooks International Standard Sizes 3.00 and 3.50.

MEASUREMENTS. To fit bust sizes 32 (34, 36) in.; hip size 34 (36, 38) in.; length of top 30 (30½, 31) in.; inside leg seam of trousers 28 (28½, 29) in.

TENSION. 11 sts. and 10 rows to 2 in. with No. 3.50 hook.

ABBREVIATIONS. See left.

TOP
BACK
With No. 3.00 hook, make 116 (122, 128) ch. * *
Foundation row (right side): 1 d.c. in 2nd ch. from hook, 1 d.c. in each ch. to end, turn: 115 (121, 127) sts.
Next row: 1 d.c. in first st., 1 d.c. in each st. to end, turn. Rep. this row twice more.
Change to No. 3.50 hook and work in patt. as follows:
1st row: 3 ch., miss first 2 sts., 1 h.tr. in next st., * 1 ch., miss next st., 1 h.tr. in next st., rep. from * to end, turn.
2nd row: 1 d.c. in first st., * 1 d.tr. in next ch. sp., 1 d.c. in next h.tr., rep. from * to end, working last d.c. in 2nd of 3 ch., turn.
These 2 rows form patt.
Work straight in patt. until Back measures 3 in. from start, ending with a 2nd patt. row. * *
Dec. row: 3 ch., miss first 2 sts., 1 h.tr. in next st., (1 ch., miss next st., 1 h.tr. in next st.) 8 times, 1 ch., miss next 3 sts., 1 h.tr. in next st., patt. to last 22 sts., 1 ch., miss 3 sts., 1 h.tr. in next st., patt. to end: 111 (117, 123) sts.
Work 13 rows straight in patt.
Work dec. row again: 107 (113, 119) sts.
Rep. last 14 rows twice more: 99 (105, 111) sts.
Work 7 rows straight.
Work dec. row again.
Rep. last 8 rows once more: 91 (97, 103) sts.
Work straight in patt. on these sts. until Back measures 23 in. from start, ending with right side facing.
Keeping continuity of patt., shape armholes as follows:
1st row: s.s. across 4 sts., patt. to last 4 sts., turn.
2nd row: in patt.
3rd row: s.s. across 2 sts., patt. to last 2 sts., turn.
Rep. 2nd and 3rd rows until 59 (61, 63) sts. remain.
Work straight until Back measures 30 (30½, 31) in.
Fasten off.

RIGHT FRONT

With No. 3.00 hook, make 58 (60, 64) ch. and work as Back from ** to **: 57 (59, 63) sts.
Dec. row: patt. to last 22 sts., 1 ch., miss next 3 sts., 1 h.tr. in next st., patt. to end: 55 (57, 61) sts.
Work 13 rows straight.
Work dec. row again: 53 (55, 59) sts.
Rep. last 14 rows twice more: 49 (51, 55) sts.
Work 7 rows straight.
Work dec. row again.
Rep. last 8 rows once more: 45 (47, 51) sts.
Work straight on these sts. until Front measures same as Back to start of armhole shaping, ending with right side facing.
Keeping continuity of patt., shape armhole as follows:
1st row: patt. to last 4 sts., turn.
2nd row: in patt.
3rd row: patt. to last 2 sts., turn.
Rep. 2nd and 3rd rows until 29 (29, 31) sts. remain.
Work 7 (5, 5) rows straight.

Shape Neck. Next row: s.s. across 10 sts., patt. to end.
Next row: in patt.
Next row: s.s. across 2 sts., patt. to end.
Rep. last 2 rows until 11 sts. remain.
Work straight until Front measures same as Back.
Fasten off.

LEFT FRONT

Work as for Right Front, reversing all shapings.

TO COMPLETE

Block out to shape and press very lightly using a cool iron and dry cloth. Join shoulder seams.

Front Border. With right side facing and No. 3.00 hook, work in d.c. up right front edge, round neck and down left front edge, turn and work 3 rows more in d.c., inc. or dec. where necessary to ensure Border lies flat.
Fasten off.
Work buttonloops on Right Front as follows:
To make a loop: join in yarn 3 in. down from neck edge and make 6 ch., miss 4 sts., s.s. in next st., turn, work 7 d.c. in 6 ch. sp., s.s. to main border.
Fasten off.
Make 4 more loops, leaving 4 in. between each one.

Armhole Border. With right side facing for first row and No. 3.00 hook, work 5 rows d.c. as for front border.
Join side seams and armhole borders.
Press seams only.
Attach buttons.

TROUSERS
RIGHT LEG

With No. 3.50 hook, make 113 (119, 125) ch. and work foundation row as on Back of Top: 112 (118, 124) sts.
Work 3 rows more in d.c.
Next row: 3 ch. to form first st., miss first st., * 1 tr. in next st., rep. from * to end, turn.
Rep. this row until work measures 25½ (26, 26½) in. from start, ending with right side facing.
Inc. row: 3 ch., 1 tr. in first st., work to last st., 2 tr. in last st., turn: 114 (120, 126) sts.
Next row: in tr.
Rep. these 2 rows 3 times more: 120 (126, 132) sts.

Shape Top. 1st row: s.s. across 2 sts., work to last 2 sts., turn.
2nd row: s.s. across first st., work to last but 1 st., turn.
Rep. 2nd row until 100 (106, 112) sts. remain.
Work 1 row straight.
Now keep front edge straight and dec. at back edge only (end of next row, beg. of next row on Left Leg) on next and every following alt. row until 89 (94, 99) sts. remain.
Work 2 rows straight (1 row on Left Leg), thus ending at back edge.
Change to No. 3.00 hook and shape back as follows:
1st row: 1 d.c. in next 60 (65, 70) sts., turn.
2nd and every alt. row: in d.c. to end, turn.
3rd row: 1 d.c. in next 48 (52, 56) sts., turn.
5th row: 1 d.c. in next 36 (39, 42) sts., turn.
7th row: 1 d.c. in next 24 (26, 28) sts., turn.
9th row: 1 d.c. in next 12 (13, 14) sts., turn.
11th row: in d.c. across all sts.
Work 10 rows straight in d.c.
Fasten off.

LEFT LEG

Work as for Right Leg reversing all shapings.

TO COMPLETE

Press using a cool iron and dry cloth.
Join front, back and leg seams.
Make herringbone casing at waist for elastic. Insert elastic.
Join ends. Press seams.

Pink and white beach set
Illustrated in colour on page 56

MATERIALS. For cape: 5 (6, 6) balls Wendy Invitation Cotton in main shade and 7 (8, 8) balls in a contrasting shade (or any mediumweight cotton to give tension indicated below). One crochet hook International Standard Size 3.00. 1½ yards cord. **For bikini:** 5 (5, 7) balls Wendy Invitation Cotton in main shade and 1 ball in contrasting shade. One crochet hook International Standard Size 3.00. Waist length narrow elastic. Two hooks and eyes.

MEASUREMENTS. To fit bust size 32 (34, 36) in. and hip size 34 (36, 38) in.; length of Cape 20½ in.

TENSION. 10 sts. to 1½ in. and 5 rows to 1¾ in. over Cape patt.; 5 sts. to 1 in. over d.c.

ABBREVIATIONS. See opposite; M., main shade; C., contrasting shade.

CAPE (worked from top downwards)

Note. This garment can also be worn as a skirt if preferred.

With C. commence with 194 (209, 224) ch.

Foundation row: 1 tr. into the 3rd ch. from hook, 1 tr. into next ch., * miss 3 ch., 2 tr., 2 ch. and 2 tr. into next ch., miss 3 ch., 1 tr. into each of next 3 ch.; rep. from * to end.

Patt. row: 2 ch., 1 tr. into each of next 2 tr., 2 tr., 2 ch. and 2 tr. into 2 ch. sp., * 3 tr. into next gr. of tr., 2 tr., 2 ch. and 2 tr. into next 2 ch. sp.; rep. from * ending with 1 tr. into each of last 2 tr., 1 tr. into top of turning ch. Rep. last row once.

Now start to inc.: where there is an uneven number of tr. in the gr. work 2 tr. into the centre one; where there is an even number work 1 extra tr. through the centre of gr.

For size 32 only. Next row: patt., inc. 1 tr. in the 2nd, 5th, 8th, 10th, 11th, 13th, 16th and 19th tr. grs.

For sizes 34 and 36 only. Next row: patt., inc. 1 tr. in the 2nd (3rd) and every foll. 3rd gr.

For all sizes. Keeping the tr. grs. correct work 1 more row. Change to M. Now work 5 rows in each colour alternately and at the same time cont. to inc. as follows, working the incs. on the first row of each colour change.

For size 32 only. On next and every foll. alt. inc. row, inc. 1 tr. in the 2nd, 5th, 8th, 13th, 16th, 19th grs. only. On other inc. rows inc. as before.

For sizes 34 and 36 only. Inc. on same grs. as first inc. row.

For all sizes. Cont. to inc. until there are 12 trs. in the inc. grs. Work 5 rows straight in C. Fasten off.

The wrap-around skirt doubles as a cape, if wished.

Border. With C. and right side facing, beg. at top of left front edge and into each stripe down the side work 3 tr. to centre row, then into centre row work 2 tr., 2 ch. and 2 tr., then work 3 more tr. to end of stripe. Cont. to lower edge, then into the corner work 2 tr., 2 ch. and 2 tr., then cont. along lower edge working the 12 tr. grs. as before, work the second corner in the same way, then cont. up the 2nd side as for the first.

Work 4 more rows in patt. Fasten off.

To Make Up. Press with a warm iron over a damp cloth. Thread cord through the patt. holes at the top. Tie each end of cord 3 in. from the end and fringe out to form a tassel.

BIKINI BRIEFS

FRONT

With M., commence with 15 ch.

1st row: miss first ch., 1 d.c. into each of next 14 ch., 1 ch.; turn.

Patt. row: 1 d.c. into 2nd st., 1 d.c. into each st. to end, 1 ch., turn.

Rep. patt. row 12 times more.

Now inc. 1 st. (by working 2 d.c. into the same st.) at each end of the next and every foll. 3rd row until there are 22 sts.

Inc. 1 d.c. at each end of the next and every foll. row until there are 36 (40, 44) sts. ending last row with 4 ch.

Next row: 1 d.c. into 2nd ch. from hook, 1 d.c. into each of next 2 ch., patt. to end, 4 ch.; turn.

Rep. last row 5 times more ending last row with 5 ch.

Next row: 1 d.c. into 2nd ch. from hook, 1 d.c. into each of next 3 ch., patt. to end, 5 ch.; turn.

Work straight for 3½ in. in d.c.

Rep. last row once ending with 1 ch. Fasten off.

BACK

Return to the 14 ch. at the beg. of Front. Join M. and work 6 rows of d.c. along other edge of ch. Cont. in d.c., inc. 1 d.c. at each end of every row until there are 42 (46, 50) d.c. Inc. 1 d.c. at each end of every alt. row until there are 62 (66, 70) d.c.

Work straight in d.c. for 3½ in. Fasten off.

TO COMPLETE

Sides. With M., work 22 d.c. along one straight 3½ in. side edge of Back.

Next row: 2 ch., 1 tr. into 2nd st., * miss 3 d.c., 2 tr., 1 ch. and 2 tr. into next d.c., miss 3 d.c., 1 tr. into each of next 3 d.c.; rep. from * once.

Rep. the last row 4 times more. Fasten off.

Work other side of Back and sides of Front in same way.

Leg Borders. With M. work 112 (122, 132) d.c. round one leg edge.

With C. work 2 rows in patt. as for the sides. Fasten off. Work round other leg edge in same way.

To Make Up. Press with a warm iron over a damp cloth. Join side seams. Put elastic round waist and hold in place with herringbone casing.

BRA

CUPS (make 2 alike)

With M. commence with 4 ch. and join into a circle with a s.s.

1st round: 8 d.c. into the circle, s.s. into the first d.c., 1 ch.; turn and work in the opposite direction (beg. every round in this way).

Next round: 2 d.c. into 2nd d.c., * 1 d.c. into next d.c., 2 d.c. into next d.c.: rep. from * to end, s.s. into first d.c., 1 ch.; turn: 12 d.c.

Next round: 1 d.c. into 2nd d.c., * 2 d.c. into next d.c., 1 d.c. into each of next 2 d.c.; rep. from * twice, 2 d.c. into last d.c., s.s. into first d.c., 1 ch.; turn: 16 d.c.

Cont. to inc. 4 d.c. in every round, working these between the incs. of the round before until there are 80 (88, 96) d.c.
Next row: work 14 (16, 18) d.c.; turn.
Work on these d.c. only, working 1 d.c. fewer at each end of every row until only 2 d.c. are worked. Fasten off.

TO COMPLETE

Back Strap and Joining Cups. With M. make 36 (38, 40) ch., then work 8 (9, 10) d.c. along one side of the triangle part of first Cup, work 18 (20, 22) d.c. round edge of circle part of first Cup, count 18 (20, 22) d.c. round circle part of 2nd Cup counting from the triangle, then work from this part round to triangle working 1 d.c. into each d.c., work 8 (9, 10) d.c. along side of triangle, then make 36 (38, 40) ch. Work 8 rows in d.c. across all sts. including the ch. Fasten off.

Neck Strap. Join M. with a s.s. to one Cup at the 14th (16th, 18th) d.c. from free side of triangle, make 98 ch., s.s. into the 14th (16th, 18th) d.c. from the triangle on the 2nd Cup, s.s. into next d.c. towards the centre, turn; 1 d.c. into each ch., s.s. into next d.c. towards the centre of first Cup; turn.
Rep. last row 5 times more, reading d.c. for ch. on strap. Fasten off.

Borders. With C. beg. at one end of back strap, join with 2 ch., 1 tr. into each of the next 2 d.c., *miss 3 d.c., 2 tr., 2 ch. and 2 tr. into next d.c., miss 3 ch., 1 tr. into each of the next 3 d.c.; rep. from * working round outer edge of first cup, neck strap and 2nd cup, and along other back strap, 1 ch.; turn.

Next row: 1 tr. into each of the 3 tr. of gr., and 2 tr., 2 ch. and 2 tr. into each 2 ch. sp. along row, ending with 3 tr. at the end of strap. Fasten off.

Join C. to centre of V then working round inner edge of cups and neck strap, work 1 tr. in centre, * miss 3 d.c., 2 tr., 2 ch. and 2 tr. into next d.c., miss 3 d.c., 1 tr. into each of next 3 d.c.; rep. from *, for size 32 only missing 2 d.c. instead of 3 at the join of strap, for size 34 only missing 4 d.c. instead of 3 at the join of strap, for size 36 only missing 1 d.c. instead of 3 at the join of strap, ending with a s.s. at the centre of V. Fasten off.

To Make Up. Press with a warm iron over a damp cloth. Sew 2 hooks and eyes to the ends of back strap.

Motif waistcoat
Illustrated in colour on page 57

MATERIALS. 6 balls Hayfield Beaulon 4-ply in main shade, 2 balls in each of first and 2nd contrasting shades and 1 ball in each of 3rd and 4th contrasting shades (or any 4-ply yarn to give tension indicated below). One crochet hook International Standard Size 4.00. Four medium buttons.

MEASUREMENTS. To fit bust size 34 in.; length 27 in.

TENSION. 1 motif measures 4 in. square.

ABBREVIATIONS. See page 36; M., main shade; A., first contrasting shade; B., 2nd contrasting shade; C., 3rd contrasting shade; D., 4th contrasting shade.

FULL SQUARES (make 22 in D., A. and M. and 18 in C., B. and M.)
With D. commence with 8 ch. and s.s. to first ch. to form a ring.
1st round: 3 ch., leaving last loop of each on hook work 2 d.tr., y.o.h. and drawn through all 3 loops on hook, 5 ch., * leaving last loop of each on hook work 3 d.tr., y.o.h. and draw through all 4 loops (1 cl. made), 5 ch.; rep. from * 6 times, s.s. to beg. of round: 8 petals.
Break D. and change to A.
2nd round: into each of the 8 5-ch. loops work 1 d.c., 1 h.tr., 1 tr., 1 d.tr., 1 ch., 1 d.tr., 1 tr., 1 h.tr., 1 d.c. Break A. and change to M.
3rd round: join yarn to centre ch. of petal point with an s.s., * 4 ch., 1 d.tr. in between the 2 d.c. of previous row, 4 ch., 1 d.c. into centre ch. of next petal point; rep. from * all round.
4th round: 2 ch., 3 tr. into 4-ch. loop, 4 tr. into next 4-ch. loop, 3 ch. to form corner, * 4 tr. into each of next 4 4-ch. loops, 3 ch.; rep. from * twice, 4 tr. into each of next 2 4-ch. loops, s.s. to beg. of round.
Fasten off.

HALF SQUARES (make 8 in C., B. and M. and 1 in D., A. and M.)
With C. commence with 8 ch. and s.s. to form a ring.
1st row: 6 ch., * 1 cl. of 3 d.tr., 5 ch.; rep. from * twice, 1 cl. of 3 d.tr., 6 ch., s.s. into ring. Change to B.

2nd row: join yarn to 3rd ch. of first 6 of first row, 4 ch., 1 tr., 1 h.tr., 1 d.c. into loop, * into each 5-ch. loop work 1 d.c., 1 h.tr., 1 tr., 1 d.tr., 1 ch., 1 d.tr., 1 tr., 1 h.tr., 1 d.c; into last loop work 1 d.c., 1 h.tr., 1 tr. and 1 d.tr. Fasten off. Change to M.
3rd row: 1 d.c. into 4th ch. of 2nd row, * 4-ch., 1 d.tr. between 2 d.c. of 2nd row, 4 ch., 1 d.c. into petal point; rep. from * 3 times, working last d.c. into top of d.tr. Fasten off.
4th row: join M. with an s.s. into 2nd 4-ch. loop of 3rd row, 3 ch., 3 tr. into loop, 4 tr. into each of next 2 4-ch. loops, 3 ch., 4 tr. into each of next 4 4-ch. loops, 3 ch., work 4 tr. down side of d.tr. of 2nd row, work 4 tr. into last 3 ch. of first row, work 4 tr. into centre ring, work 4 tr. into first 3 ch. of first row, work 4 tr. into first 4 ch. of 2nd row, 3 ch., 4 tr. into next 4-ch. loop of 3rd row, 3 ch., s.s. to 3rd ch. of first set of 4 tr. Fasten off.

TO COMPLETE
Join squares and half squares as shown in diagram below. Join side seams.
With M. work 2 rows of d.c. round each armhole and round neck, front and lower edge. Link each pair of buttons with a crochet ch., 2 in. long, and use to fasten centre front edges of waistcoat, at points of motifs.

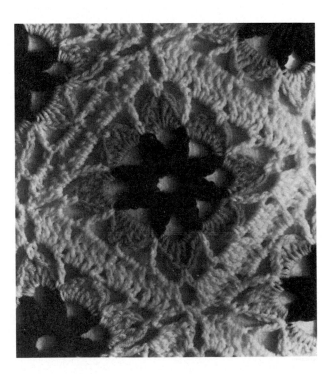

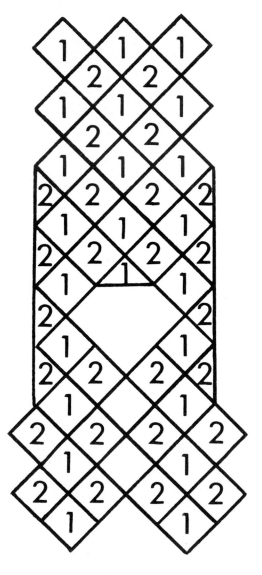

1 = Pink and Viola
2 = Blue and Turquoise

Laced long dress

Illustrated in colour on page 52

MATERIALS. 19 balls Lister Bel Air Starspun in main shade and 2 balls in a contrasting shade (or any mediumweight glitter yarn to give tension indicated below). Crochet hooks International Standard Sizes 3.50, 3.00 and 4.00.

MEASUREMENTS. To fit bust size 34 (36, 38) in.; length 50 in.; length of sleeve seam 17 in.

TENSION. 6 tr to 1 in. and 7 rows to 2¼ in. with No. 3.00 hook.

ABBREVIATIONS. See page 36; dec. 1 tr., work 2 tr. leaving last loop of each on hook, y.o.h. and draw through all 3 loops; M., main shade; C., contrasting shade.

BACK (worked from top downwards)
With No. 3.00 hook and M. commence with 73 (77, 81) ch.
1st row (right side): 1 tr. in 3rd ch. from hook, 1 tr. in to each ch. to end, 2 ch. (to stand as first tr. on next row); turn: 72 (76, 80) tr.
2nd row: 1 tr. into 2nd tr., 1 tr. into each tr. to end, 2 ch.; turn.
The last row forms the patt.
Rep. 2nd row 16 times.

Shape Armhole. 1st row: 1 tr. into first tr. (inc. made), 2 tr. into next tr., patt. to last 2 tr., 2 tr. into each of last 2 tr., 2 ch.; turn.
Rep. last row 6 times.
8th row: 1 tr. into first tr., 2 tr. into each of next 1 (2, 3) tr., patt. to last 2 (3, 4) tr., 2 tr. into each of last 2 (3, 4) tr., 2 ch.; turn: 104 (110, 116) tr.
Cont. straight in patt. until work measures 15 in.
With No. 3.50 hook, cont. straight until work measures 22 in.
With No. 4.00 hook cont. straight until work measures 50 in. or required length. Fasten off.

FRONT (worked from top downwards)
Left Front. With No. 3.00 hook and M. commence with 21 (23, 25) ch.
1st row: 1 tr. into 3rd ch. from hook, 1 tr. into each ch. to end, 2 ch.; turn: 20 (22, 24) tr.
2nd row: 1 tr. into 2nd tr., 1 tr. into each tr. to last tr., 2 tr. into last tr., 2 ch.; turn.
3rd row: 1 tr. into first tr., 1 tr. into each tr. to end, 2 ch.; turn.
Rep. 2nd and 3rd rows 7 times: 36 (38, 40) tr. Work 1 row.

Shape Armhole. 1st row: patt to last 2 tr., 2 tr. into each of last 2 tr., 2 ch.; turn.
2nd row: 1 tr. into first tr., 2 tr. into next tr., patt. to end, 2 ch.; turn.
Rep. last 2 rows twice, then first of them again.
8th row: 1 tr. into first tr., 2 tr. into each of next 1 (2, 3) tr., patt. to end, 2 ch.; turn: 52 (55, 58) tr.
Cont. straight in patt. until work measures 15 in. ending with a wrong-side row.

Right Front. With No. 3.00 hook and M. commence with 21 (23, 25) ch.
1st row: 1 tr. into 3rd ch. from hook 1 tr. into each ch. to end, 2 ch.; turn: 20 (22, 24) tr.
2nd row: 1 tr. into first tr., 1 tr. into each tr. to end, 2 ch.; turn.
3rd row: 1 tr. into each tr. to last tr., 2 tr. into last tr., 2 ch.; turn.
Rep. 2nd and 3rd rows 7 times: 36 (38, 40) tr. Work 1 row.

Shape Armhole. 1st row: 1 tr. into first tr., 2 tr. into next tr., patt. to end, 2 ch.; turn.
2nd row: patt. to last 2 tr., 2 tr. into each of last 2 tr., 2 ch.; turn.
Rep. last 2 rows twice, then first of them again.
8th row: patt. to last 2 (3, 4) tr., 2 tr. into each of last 2 (3, 4) tr., 2 ch.; turn: 52 (55, 58) tr.
Cont. straight in patt. until work measures same as left front.

Join Fronts. With No. 3.50 hook and right side facing, patt. across 52 (55, 58) tr. of right front, then patt. across 52 (55, 58) tr. of left front, 2 ch.; turn: 104 (110, 116) tr.
Now complete to correspond with Back.

SLEEVES (make 2 alike)
With No. 3.00 hook and M., commence with 49 (51, 53) ch. Work 6 rows in patt. as given for Back, inc. 1 tr. at each end of 3rd and 6th rows. Cont. to inc. at each end of every 3rd row until there are 72 (76, 80) tr. Work in foll. stripe patt.
4 rows in C.
2 rows in M.
4 rows in C.
6 rows in M.
These 16 rows form stripe patt.
Keeping continuity of stripe patt. cont. straight after incs. until Sleeve measures 17 in. Cont. in patt.

Shape Top. 1st row: dec. 1 tr. 2 (3, 4) times, patt. to last 5 (7, 9) tr., dec. 1 tr. 2 (3, 4) times, 1 tr. into last tr., 2 ch.; turn.
2nd row: dec. 1 tr. twice, patt. to last 5 tr., dec. 1 tr. twice, 1 tr. into last tr., 2 ch.; turn.
Rep. last row 6 times.
Next row: dec. 1 tr., patt. to last 3 tr., dec. 1 tr., 1 tr. into last tr., 2 ch.; turn.
Rep. last row 7 times.
Fasten off.

TO COMPLETE
Press each piece carefully. Sew shoulder seams, then side and sleeve seams. Sew in Sleeves. With No. 3.00 hook and M., work 1 row of d.c. round each cuff and lower and neck edges. With C., make a crochet chain 30 in. long. Thread between tr. down front edge of each Front to form a laced effect as shown in photograph on page 52. Press all seams.

Summer suit

MATERIALS. 21 (22, 23) oz. Emu Tricel in main shade and 1 oz. in a contrasting shade (or any Tricel yarn to give tension indicated below). Crochet hooks International Standard Sizes 3.00 and 3.50. Six invisible snap fasteners. One 8-in. zip fastener. 1 yard petersham ribbon 1 in. wide.

MEASUREMENTS. To fit bust size 34 (36, 38) in. and hip size 36 (38, 40) in.

TENSION. 2 blocks to about 1 in.

ABBREVIATIONS. See page 36; dec. 1 tr., leaving last loop of each on hook, work 2 tr., y.o.h. and draw through all 3 loops on hook; M., main shade; C., contrasting shade.

JACKET
BACK BODICE
With No. 3.50 hook and M., commence with 72 (78, 84) ch.
1st row: 1 tr. into 3rd ch. from hook, * 1 ch., miss 1 ch., 1 tr. into each of next 2 ch. (1 block made); rep. from * to end, 3 ch. (to stand as first tr. of next row); turn: 24 (26, 28) blocks.
Patt. row: 1 tr. into 2nd tr., * 1 ch., miss 1 ch., 1 tr. into each of next 2 tr.; rep. from * to end, 3 ch.; turn.
This row forms the patt.
1st inc. row: 1 ch., 2 tr. into next tr. (inc. made), patt. over next 5 blocks, 2 tr. into first tr. of next block, 1 ch., 1 tr. into next tr., patt. to last 7 blocks, 1 tr. into first tr., 1 ch., 2 tr. into next tr., patt. to last block, 2 tr. into first tr., 1 ch., 1 tr. into last tr., 3 ch.; turn.
2nd inc. row: 1 tr. into first tr. (with ch. making 2 tr. into same st.), patt. to single tr., 2 tr. into this tr., 1 ch., patt. to next single tr., 2 tr. into this tr., patt. to end working 2 tr. into turning ch., 3 ch.; turn.
Work 2 rows straight.
Rep. last 4 rows twice more: 36 (38, 40) blocks.
Work 12 rows straight, omitting turning ch. at end of last row.

Shape Armholes. Next row: s.s. to 4th block, 3 ch., patt. to last 3 blocks; turn.
Next row: s.s. over first block, patt. to last block, 3 ch.; turn: 28 (30, 32) blocks.
Work 18 rows straight, omitting turning ch. at end of last row.

Shape Shoulders. Next row: s.s. to 7th block, 3 ch., patt. to last 6 blocks. Break yarn.

RIGHT FRONT BODICE
With No. 3.50 hook and M. commence with 36 (39, 42) ch. Work 2 rows in patt. as given for Back.
1st inc. row: patt. over 6 blocks, 1 tr. into first tr. of next block, 1 ch., 2 tr. into next tr., patt. to last block, 2 tr. into next tr., 1 ch., 1 tr. into last tr., 3 ch.; turn.
2nd inc. row: 1 tr. into first tr. (with ch. making 2 tr. into the same st.), patt. to the single tr., 2 tr into this tr , 1 ch., patt. to end, 3 ch.; turn.
Work 2 rows straight.
Rep. last 4 rows twice: 18 (19, 20) blocks.
Work 9 rows straight.
Next row: patt. to last block, dec. 1 tr. over last 2 tr., 3 ch.; turn.
Next row: patt. to end of row.
Work 2 rows straight, omitting turning ch. at end of last row.

Shape Armhole. Next row: s.s. to 4th block, 3 ch., patt. to last block, dec. 1 tr. over last 2 tr., 3 ch.; turn.
Next row: patt. to last block, 3 ch.; turn.
Work 2 rows straight.
Next row: patt. to last block, dec. 1 tr. over last 2 tr., 3 ch.; turn.
Next row: patt. to end of row.
Work 2 rows straight.
Rep. last 4 rows twice.
Work 4 rows straight, omitting turning ch. at end of last row.

Shape Shoulder. Next row: s.s. to 5th block, 3 ch., patt. to end of row.
Break yarn.

LEFT FRONT BODICE
Work to match Right Front, reversing shapings.

LOWER JACKET
Sew up side seams and shoulder seams. With No. 3.50 hook and right side facing join M. to Left Front lower edge to work lower part of jacket in one piece.
1st row: 3 ch., 1 tr. into next ch., * 1 ch., miss 1 ch., 1 tr. into each of next 2 tr.; rep. from * to end, 3 ch.; turn: 48 (52, 56) blocks.
1st inc. row: patt. over first 6 blocks, 1 tr. into first tr., 1 ch., 2 tr. into next tr., patt. over next 4 (5, 6) blocks, 2 tr. into next tr., 1 ch., 1 tr. into next tr., 1 ch., 1 tr. into next tr., 1 ch., 2 tr. into next tr., patt. over next 5 blocks, 2 tr. into next tr., 1 ch., 1 tr. into next tr., patt. over next 10 (12, 14) blocks, 1 tr. into next tr., 1 ch., 2 tr. into next tr., patt. over next 5 blocks, 2 tr. into next tr., 1 ch., 1 tr. into next tr., 1 ch., 1 tr. into next tr., 1 ch., 2 tr. into next tr., patt. over next 4 (5, 6) blocks, 2 tr. into next tr., 1 ch., 1 tr. into next tr., patt. over next 6 blocks., 3 ch.; turn.
2nd inc. row: patt., working 2 tr. into each single tr.
Work 2 rows straight.
Next row: as first inc. row, but work 6 (7, 8) blocks instead of 4 (5, 6) blocks, 6 blocks instead of 5 blocks and 12 (14, 16) blocks instead of 10 (12, 14) blocks.
Next row: as 2nd inc. row.
Work 2 rows straight.
Rep. last 4 rows once but work 8 (9, 10) blocks instead of 6 (7, 8) blocks, 7 blocks instead of 6 blocks, and 14 (16, 18) blocks instead of 12 (14, 16) blocks; do not turn at the end of last row, and work 1 ch. instead of 3.

Edgings. Now work 118 d.c. up Right Front front edge, 30 d.c. across back neck and 118 d.c. down Left Front front edge, then cont. along lower edge working 1 d.c. into each tr. and 1 d.c. into each 1 ch. space to end, s.s. to first d.c. Fasten off. With No. 3.00 hook and C. used double, and wrong side facing, join yarn to Left Front front edge 4 rows below armhole (working towards neck), 3 ch., 1 tr. into next d.c., * miss 1 d.c., 3 ch., 1 d.c. into each of next 2 d.c., miss 1 d.c., 3 ch., 1 tr. into each of next 2 d.c.; rep. from * until the Left

Front lower corner of Jacket is reached, 1 d.c. into each d.c. up front of Jacket to joining ch., s.s. to ch. Fasten off.
With No. 3.50 hook and M. work d.c. evenly round each armhole. With No. 3.00 hook and C. used double work a row of edging as before. Sew fasteners at front of jacket.

SKIRT
BACK AND FRONT (make 2 pieces alike)
With No. 3.50 hook and M. commence with 84 (90, 96) ch. and work first 2 rows as for Jacket Back: 28 (30, 32) blocks. Work 2 rows straight.
1st inc. row: 2 tr. into 2nd tr., 1 ch., patt. over next 6 blocks, 2 tr. into next tr., 1 ch., 1 tr. into next tr., patt. over next 12 (14, 16) blocks, 1 tr. into next tr., 1 ch., 2 tr. into next tr., patt. over next 6 blocks, 2 tr. into next tr., 1 tr. into last tr., 3 ch.; turn.
2nd inc. row: 1 tr. into first tr., 1 ch., patt. to single tr., 2 tr. into this tr., 1 ch., patt. to next single tr., 2 tr. into this tr., patt. to last tr., 2 tr. into last tr., 3 ch.; turn: 32 (34, 36) blocks. Work 4 rows straight.
Cont. inc. in this way: 1 block at each end and 1 block each side of centre 12 (14, 16) blocks on next 2 rows and every foll. 5th and 6th rows until there are 72 (74, 76) blocks. Work 4 rows straight after last inc. Fasten off.

TO COMPLETE
Join side seams leaving an opening 8 in. at top left side for zip.

Waistband. Rejoin M. to waist edge. With 3.50 hook, * 1 d.c. into each of next 2 ch., miss 1 ch.; rep. from * to end. Work 7 rows of d.c. Fasten off.

Edging. Work 3 rows of d.c. along front edge of side opening to conceal zip. Insert zip. Work 1 row of d.c. along lower edge of Skirt. Fasten off.

Three-colour sweater

MATERIALS. 8 oz. Wendy Double Knit Nylonised in each of 3 contrasting colours (or any nylonised double knitting yarn to give tension indicated below). Crochet hooks International Standard Sizes 3.50 (4.00, 3.50), 4.00 (4.50, 4.00) and 4.50 (5.00, 4.50).

MEASUREMENTS. To fit bust size 34 (36/37, 38/40) in.; length 21 (21½, 22) in.; length of sleeve seam 16 in.

TENSION. 2 rows to 1 in. and 1 patt. to 1½ in. with No. 4.00 hook.

ABBREVIATIONS. See page 36; A., first colour; B., 2nd colour; C., 3rd colour.

BACK

With No. 4.00 (4.50, 4.00) hook and A., commence with 77 (77, 83) ch.

1st row (**right side**) : 1 tr. into 3rd ch. from hook, 1 tr. into each ch. to end : 76 (76, 82) sts.

2nd row : 2 ch., 1 tr. into next tr., * 5 tr. into next st. (now called 1 motif), (insert hook into next st. and draw through a loop) 5 times, y.o.h. and draw through all 6 loops ; rep. from * ending with 1 tr. into each of last 2 sts.
Join B.

1st patt. row : 2 ch., 1 tr. into next st., 1 tr. into each st. to end.

2nd patt. row : 2 ch., 1 tr. into next st., * 1 motif, (insert hook into next st. and draw through a loop) 5 times, y.o.h. and draw through all 6 loops ; rep. from * ending with 1 tr. into each of last 2 sts.

These 2 rows form patt. Work in patt. in stripes of 2 rows A., 2 rows B., 2 rows C.

Work straight until Back measures 14 in., ending with a 2nd patt. row. Break yarn.

Shape Armholes. Next row : miss 4 sts., rejoin correct yarn and work in tr. to last 4 sts ; turn.

Dec. 1 st. at each end of foll. 2 rows : 64 (64, 70) sts.

Cont. straight until armholes measure 5 (6) in., ending with a 2nd patt. row.

Next row : work across 3 patts. (3 patts., 3 patts. and 3 tr.) ; turn. Work 1 more row, then work 2 rows in d.c. Break yarn.

Next row : miss first 7 sts., rejoin correct yarn and work in d.c. to end.

Next row : work 7 (7, 9) d.c. Break yarn.

Leaving 4 patts. at centre, rejoin yarn and work 2nd side of neck to match first.

FRONT
Work as Back.

SLEEVES (make 2 alike)

With No. 4.00 (4.50, 4.00) hook and A. commence with 41 (41, 45) ch. and work in stripes in patt., inc. 1 st. at each end by working 2 sts. into first and last sts. of every 4th row 6 times, then 1 st. at each end of every alt. row 3 times, working incs. at first in tr. then gradually taking into patt : 58 (58, 64) sts. Cont. straight if necessary until Sleeve measures 16 in., ending with a 2nd patt. row. Break yarn.

Shape Top. 1st row : rejoin correct yarn to 5th st., work in tr. to last 4 sts. ; turn.

2nd row : 2 ch., miss 2 tr., 1 tr. into each of next 2 tr., work next 2 motifs of 4 tr. each, patt. to last 2 motifs, work last 2 motifs of 4 tr. each, miss 1 tr., 1 tr. into each of last 2 tr. ; turn.

3rd row : 2 ch., miss 1 tr., patt. to last tr. ; turn.

4th row : 2 ch., 1 tr. into next tr., work next 2 motifs of 3 tr. each, patt. to last 2 motifs, work last 2 motifs of 3 tr. each, 1 tr. into last tr.

5th row : as 3rd row.

6th row : 2 ch., tr. to first motif, work next 2 motifs 2 tr. each, patt. to last 2 motifs, work last 2 motifs 2 tr. each, tr. to end.

7th row : as 3rd row.

For size 38/40 only. Work 1 more row in tr.

For all sizes. Next row : work in d.c., dec. 1 st. at each end of row.

Next row : s.s. over 3 sts., patt. to last 3 sts. Fasten off.

TO COMPLETE

Collar. With No. 4.00 (4.50, 4.00) hook and A., beg. at centre back and tr. 15 (15, 16) sts. round neck to shoulder, 18 (18, 20) sts. from shoulder to centre front, 18 (18, 20) sts. to second shoulder and 15 (15, 16) sts. to centre back. Work 7 in. in patt., working last 2 rows with No. 4.50 (5.00, 4.50) hook. Fasten off and join tog. edges of Collar.

With No. 3.50 (4.00, 3.50) hook and B. work 3 rows of d.c. round bottom edge of Sweater and Sleeves.

Pillbox hat and sweater
Also illustrated in colour on page 53

MATERIALS. 9 (9, 10) balls Wendy Invitation Cotton in main shade and 3 balls in a contrasting shade (or any medium-weight cotton to give tension indicated below). One crochet hook International Standard Size 2.50. Small quantity buckram. ½ yard lining material. One 4-in. zip fastener.

MEASUREMENTS. Hat : to fit head size 22 in. **Sweater :** to fit bust size 34 (36, 38) in. ; length 17 (17½, 18) in.

TENSION. 6½ sts. and 6 rows to 1 in. over rounds of d.c.

ABBREVIATIONS. See page 36 ; dec. 1, leaving last loop of each on hook work next 2 sts., y.o.h. and draw through all 3 loops on hook ; M., main shade ; C., contrasting shade.

Note. When working crochet in 2 colours is it essential that the 2nd half of the preceding stitch should be worked in the colour of the next stitch, otherwise the effect will be patchy i.e. when working 2 black sts. followed by 2 white, the first half of the 2nd st. must be worked in black and the 2nd half of this st. in white. The 4th st must be worked with the first half white and the 2nd half black.

HAT

With M. commence with 6 ch. and join into a ring with s.s.

1st round: 12 d.c. into ring, s.s. into first d.c.

2nd round: * 2 d.c. into each of next 2 sts., 1 d.c. into next st.; rep. from * twice, 2 d.c. into each of next 3 sts., s.s. into first d.c.: 21 sts.

3rd round: * 1 d.c. into each of next 2 sts., 2 d.c. into next st.; rep. from * 6 times, s.s. into first d c.: 28 sts.

4th round: * 1 d.c. into each of next 3 sts., 2 d.c. into next st.; rep. from * 6 times, s.s. into first d.c.: 35 sts.

5th round: * 1 d.c. into each of next 4 sts., 2 d.c. into next st.; rep. from * 6 times, s.s. into first d.c.: 42 sts.

Cont. inc. 7 sts. every round in this way, working 1 more st. between incs. each time, until there are 168 sts.

Next round: * 1 d.c. into each of next 83 sts., 2 d.c. into next st.; rep. from * once, s.s. into first d.c.: 170 sts.

Next round: work in d.c.

Change to C. and work 3 rounds straight in d.c.

Now work in M. and C. in rounds of d.c.

1st round: * 1 C., 9 M.; rep. from * 16 times, s.s. to first d.c.

2nd round: * 2 C., 7 M., 1 C.; rep. from * 16 times, s.s. to first d.c.

3rd round: * 3 C., 5 M., 1 C.; rep. from * 16 times, s.s. to first d.c.

4th round: * 4 C., 3 M., 2 C.; rep. from * 16 times, s.s. to first d.c.

5th round: * 5 C., 1 M., 4 C.; rep. from * 16 times, s.s. to first d.c.

6th round: as 4th round.

7th round: as 3rd round.

8th round: as 2nd round.

9th round: as first round.

10th round: with C. to end.

11th to 19th rounds: as first to 9th rounds.

20th round: as 10th round.

21st round: with C., * 1 d.c. into each of next 6 d.c., dec. 1 d.c. over next 2 d.c.; rep. from * 20 times, 1 d.c. into each of last 2 d.c., s.s. into first d.c.

22nd round: with C., * 1 d.c. into each of next 5 d.c., dec. 1 d.c. over next 2 d.c.; rep. from * 20 times, 1 d.c. into each of last 2 d.c., s.s. into first d.c.

SWEATER
MAIN PIECE

With C. commence with 191 (201, 211) ch.

1st row: 1 d.c. into 2nd ch. from hook, 1 d.c. into each ch. to end: 190 (200, 210) d.c.

Break yarn, rejoin at beg. of row and work 1 row in d.c. with C. Rep. this row. Now work 19 rows in patt. as for lower part of Hat (brim), breaking yarn at end of every row and rejoining at beg. Then work 3 rows in C. in same way.

Now change to M. and work a row of d.c. and join the 2 ends of row with a s.s. Place a marker of contrasting coloured thread at join and at opposite side of work. Now work in rounds in d.c. On next round work twice into st. on either side of each marker (thus inc. 4 sts.), then work 2 rows straight. Rep. these 3 rows 11 times more: 238 (248, 258) sts.

Shape Armholes. Next round: work to within 5 sts. of first marker; turn then work 5 ch., 1 d.c. into 4th st. from hook 21 (22, 23) times; turn.

Next row: sl. st. to centre of first ch.-loop, 5 ch., 1 d.c. into next space to end of row. Rep. this row until there are 19 (19, 19) patts.

Work straight in this patt. until work measures 14 (14½, 15) in. from beg.

Shape Neck. Patt. to within 1½ in. of centre (7 patts.); turn and sl. st. to centre of first ch.-loop, (5 ch., 1 d.c. into next space) to end of row. Turn and patt. across row to centre of last ch.-loop, turn, sl.st. to centre of ch.-loop then patt. back. Rep. last 2 rows twice more. Fasten off. Work up second shoulder to match, reversing shapings.

Now rejoin cotton to 5 sts. beyond marker and d.c. to within 2 sts. of 2nd marker, then work in patt. as for first half of sweater, which was for back, but in this case working only 6 rows in patt. Now shape for neck exactly as for back and when the 8 rows of shaping are completed work up straight until you have worked 25 rows of this openwork patt. and patt. matches back exactly. Fasten off and work second shoulder to match. Slip st. shoulders together.

TO COMPLETE

Press work under damp cloth.

Edgings. With C. work 80 d.c. all round one armhole then work 3 more rounds in d.c., dec. 2 sts. at bottom of armhole on 2nd and 4th rounds. Fasten off. Work round second armhole in same way. With C. work 70 d.c. round back of neck and 100 d.c. round front of neck. Work 1 further round in d.c. with C. Cont. in rounds of d.c. as follows:

1st round: * 1 C., 9 M.; rep. from * 16 times.

2nd round: * 3 C., 7 M., rep. from * 16 times.

3rd round: * 5 C., 5 M.; rep. from * 16 times.

4th round: * 7 C., 3 M.; rep. from * 16 times.

5th round: * 3 C., with C. dec. 1 st. over next 2 sts., 4 C., 1 M.; rep. from * 16 times.

6th round: with C. to end.

7th round: with C., * 1 d.c. into each of next 8 d.c., dec. 1 st. over next 2 sts.; rep. from * 16 times.

Press these edgings. Insert zip in side opening. Press.

To Make Up Hat. Press well under damp cloth. Cut a piece of buckram about 3 in. deep — or desired depth — and length to fit head and join into a ring. Cut a length of lining material about 1 in. longer and a circle of lining material to fit crown of hat. St. circle of lining in place to inside of hat. Slip st. buckram inside brim of hat firmly, then join lining strip into a ring, and slip st. to inside of Hat over buckram, turning in raw edges of lining.

Mini, midi or maxi waistcoat
Midi and maxi versions illustrated in colour on page 49

MATERIALS. For mini waistcoat: 10 (11, 12) balls Robin Tricel-Nylon Perle double knitting (or any double knitting yarn to give tension indicated below). Crochet hooks International Standard Sizes 4.00, 3.50. **For midi waistcoat:** 21 (23, 25) balls of Robin Tricel-Nylon Perle double knitting. Crochet hooks International Standard Sizes 4.50, 4.00, and 3.50. **For maxi waistcoat:** 31 (33, 35) balls Robin Tricel-Nylon Perle double knitting. Crochet hooks International Standard Sizes 5.00, 4.50, 4.00 and 3.50.

MEASUREMENTS. to fit bust size 34 (36, 38) in.; length of Mini Waistcoat 16 in.; length of Midi Waistcoat 43 in.; length of Maxi Waistcoat 56 in.

TENSION. 9 d.tr. and 4 rows to $2\frac{1}{4}$ in. over patt. with No. 4.00 hook.

ABBREVIATIONS. See page 36.

ALL VERSIONS
BACK (worked from top downwards)
With No. 4.00 hook make 6 ch. and fasten off.
With No. 4.00 hook commence with 52 (54, 56) ch.
1st row: 1 d.c. into 2nd ch. from hook, 1 d.c. into each of next 2 ch., 1 h.tr. into each of next 3 ch., 1 tr. into each of next 3 ch., 1 d.tr. into each of next 2 (3, 4) ch., 1 tr. into next ch., 1 h.tr. into next ch., 1 d.c. into each of next 25 ch., 1 h.tr. into next ch., 1 tr. into next ch., 1 d.tr. into each of next 2 (3, 4) ch., 1 tr. into each of next 3 ch., 1 h.tr. into each of next 3 ch., 1 d.c. into each of last 3 ch., 3 ch.; turn.
1st patt. row (right side): (y.o.h., insert hook into 2nd st., y.o.h. and draw through loop, y.o.h. and draw through 2 loops on hook) 3 times into same st., y.o.h. and draw through all 4 loops on hook, 1 ch. (1 cl. made), * miss 1 st., 1 cl. into next st.; rep. from * ending with 1 tr. into last st., 4 ch.; turn: 24 (25, 26) cls.
2nd patt. row: 1 d.tr. into 2nd st., 1 d.tr. into st., ending with 1 d.tr. into top of turning ch., 3 ch.; turn.
The last 2 rows form the patt. Rep. the 2 patt. rows until armholes measure 5 (6, 6) in. ending with a first patt. row.

Shape Armholes. Next row: 2 d.tr. into 2nd st., 1 d.tr. into st., ending with 2 d.tr. into top of turning ch., 3 ch.; turn.
Next row: 1 cl. into first st., * miss 1 d.tr., 1 cl. into next d.tr.; rep. from * ending with 1 tr. into top of turning ch., 4 ch.; turn: 26 (27, 28) cls.
Next row: 2 d.tr. into 2nd st., 1 d.tr. into each st., ending with 2 d.tr. into top of turning ch., 9 (9, 11) ch.; turn.
Next row: 1 cl. into 4th ch. from hook, * miss 1 ch., 1 cl. into next ch.; rep. from * 1 (1, 2) times more, ** miss 1 ch., 1 cl. into next d.tr.; rep. from ** to end, join in 6 ch. made at beg., miss top of turning ch., 1 cl. into first ch., * miss 1 ch., 1 cl. into next ch.; rep. from * ending with 1 tr. into last ch., 4 ch.; turn.
*** Work in patt. until Back measures 12 in. from shoulders. Change to No. 3.50 hook and work in patt. until Back measures 16 in. from shoulders, ending with a first patt. row.
For Mini Waistcoat only. Fasten off.
For Midi and Maxi Waistcoats only. Change to No. 4.00 hook and work until Back measures 24 in. from shoulder, change to No. 4.50 hook and work until Back measures 43 in. from shoulder, ending with a first patt. row.
For Midi Waistcoat only. Fasten off.
For Maxi Waistcoat only. Change to No. 5.00 hook and work until Back measures 56 in. from shoulder, or length required, ending with a first patt. row. Fasten off.

LEFT FRONT (worked from top downwards)
With No. 4.00 hook make 6 ch. and fasten off.
With No. 4.00 hook commence with 12 (13, 14) ch.

The mini version of the waistcoat

1st row: 1 d.c. into 2nd ch. from hook, 1 d.c. into each of next 2 ch., 1 h.tr. into each of next 3 ch., 1 tr. into each of next 3 ch., 1 d.tr. into each of last 2 (3, 4) ch., 3 ch.; turn.
Next row: 1 cl. into 2nd st., * miss 1 st., 1 cl. into next st.; rep. from * ending with 1 tr. into last st., 4 ch.; turn: 5 (5, 6) cls.

Shape Neck. Next row: 1 d.tr. into 2nd st., 1 d.tr. into each st., ending with 2 d.tr. into top of turning ch., 3 ch.; turn.
Next row: 1 cl. into first st., * miss 1 d.tr., 1 cl. into next d.tr.; rep. from * ending with 1 tr. into top of turning ch., 4 ch.; turn: 6 (6, 7) cls.
Next row: 1 d.tr. into 2nd st., 1 d.tr. into each st., ending with 2 d.tr. into top of turning ch., 12 (14, 14) ch.; turn.
Next row: 1 cl. into 5th ch. from hook, * miss 1 ch., 1 cl. into next ch.; rep. from * 2 (3, 3) times, ** miss 1 ch., 1 cl. into next d.tr.; rep. from ** ending with 1 tr. into top of turning ch., 4 ch.; turn: (11, 12, 13) cls.
Rep. the 2 patt. rows until armhole measures approx. 5 (6, 6) in., as on Back, ending with a first patt. row and turning with 4 ch.

Shape Armhole. Next row: 2 d.tr. into 2nd st., 1 d.tr. into each st., ending with 1 tr. into top of turning ch., 3 ch.; turn.
Next row: 1 cl. into 2nd st., * miss 1 d.tr., 1 cl. into next d.tr.; rep. from * ending with 1 tr. into top of turning ch., 4 ch.; turn.
Next row: 2 d.tr. into 2nd st., 1 d.tr. into each st., ending with 1 d.tr. into top of turning ch., 3 ch.; turn.
Next row: 1 cl. into 2nd st., * miss 1 d.tr., 1 cl. into next d.tr.; rep. from * to end, miss top of turning ch., join in 6 ch. made at beg., 1 cl. into first ch., ** miss 1 ch., 1 cl. into next ch.; rep. from ** ending with 1 tr. into last ch., 4 ch.; turn.
Complete as Back from ***.

Back view of the midi length waistcoat.

RIGHT FRONT (worked from top downwards)
With No. 4.00 hook make 9 (11, 11) ch. and fasten off.
With No. 4.00 hook commence with 14 (15, 16) ch.
1st row: 1 d.tr. into 5th ch. from hook, 1 d.tr. into next 0 (1, 2) ch., 1 tr. into each of next 3 ch., 1 h.tr. into each of next 3 ch., 1 d.c. into each of last 3 ch., 3 ch.; turn.
Next row: 1 cl. into 2nd st., * miss 1 st., 1 cl. into next st.; rep. from * ending with 1 tr. into top of turning ch., 4 ch.; turn: 5 (5, 6) cls.

Shape Neck. Next row: 2 d.tr. into 2nd st., 1 d.tr. into each st.; ending with 1 tr. into top of turning ch., 3 ch.; turn.
Next row: 1 cl. into 2nd st., * miss 1 d.tr., 1 cl. into next d.tr.; rep. from * ending with 1 tr. into top of turning ch., 4 ch.; turn: 6 (6, 7) cls.
Next row: 2 d.tr. into 2nd st., 1 d.tr. into each st., ending with 1 d.tr. into top of turning ch., 3 ch.; turn.
Next row: 1 cl. into 2nd st., * miss 1 st., 1 cl. into next st.; rep. from * to turning ch., miss turning ch., join 9 (11, 11) ch. made at beg., 1 cl. into first ch., ** miss 1 ch., 1 cl. into next ch.; rep. from ** ending with 1 tr. into last ch., 4 ch.; turn: 11 (12, 13) cls.
Rep. the 2 patt. rows until same number of rows have been worked on as Left Front to beg. of armhole shaping, ending with a first patt. row and turning with 4 ch.

Shape Armhole. Next row: 1 d.tr. into 2nd st., 1 d.tr. into each st., ending with 2 d.tr. into top of turning ch., 2 ch.; turn.
Next row: 1 cl. into first st., * miss 1 d.tr., 1 cl. into next d.tr.; rep. from * ending with 1 tr. into top of turning ch., 4 ch.; turn.
Next row: 1 d.tr. into 2nd st., 1 d.tr. into each st., ending with 2 d.tr. into top of turning ch., 9 (9, 11) ch.; turn.
Next row: 1 cl. into 4th ch. from hook, * miss 1 ch., 1 cl. into next ch.; rep. from * 1 (1, 2) times more, miss 1 ch., 1 cl. into next d.tr., ** miss 1 d.tr., 1 cl. into next d.tr.; rep. from ** to end, 4 ch.; turn.
Complete as Back from ***.

TO COMPLETE
Pin out and press work lightly on wrong side using a warm iron over a damp cloth. Join shoulder and side seams.

Edging. With No. 3.50 hook and right side facing, join yarn at side seam of one armhole, 2 ch., then work a row of h.tr. evenly around armhole. Work 2 more rows of h.tr. Fasten off. Work 3 rows round other armhole.
With right side facing and No. 3.50 hook join yarn at lower edge of Right Front and work 3 rows of h.tr. evenly up front edge, around neck and down front edge of Left Front. Fasten off.
With wrong side facing and with No. 4.00 hook, join yarn at lower edge of Right Front and work 1 row of d.c. evenly along lower edge.
Change to No. 3.50 hook and work picot edging.
Next row: 1 ch., * miss 1 d.c., work 1 s.s., 3 ch. and 1 s.s. into next d.c.; rep. from * ending with miss 1 d.c., 1 d.c. into last d.c. Fasten off.
Press seams and edging lightly.

Opposite: *the casual-style waistcoat in its midi and maxi versions – instructions start on page 47.*

Chapter three
EMBROIDERY

Embroidery – the art of decorative stitchery – dates from very early times, and museums in all parts of the world show examples of fine historical pieces. Styles of embroidery have varied through the centuries and from one country to another, but the basic techniques have remained the same – these basic techniques and stitches are explained here, and a selection of designs for you to make up show how the different stitches can be used. From here you will no doubt go on to design your own embroideries – for fashion accessories, for the home, or for church.

EQUIPMENT
Needles

The ideal needle for embroidery work should pierce the fabric easily and make a large enough hole for the thread to pull through the fabric smoothly. The thread should also move through the eye of the needle freely. Never use a crooked needle for this will make a crooked stitch.

Sharps are ordinary sewing needles which are used in embroidery with mercerised cotton thread or a single strand of stranded cotton.

Crewel needles are long and sharp and have large eyes. They are used with most embroidery threads – stranded cotton, *coton à broder*, pearl cotton No. 5 and No. 8. Choose a size with a large eye, such as No. 5, when working with six strands of stranded cotton or with pearl cotton No. 5.

Chenille needles are also sharp and have large eyes, but they are slightly shorter than crewel needles. Use the No. 19 size with soft embroidery thread or tapestry wool.

Tapestry needles are used for canvas work and also for counted-thread embroidery on coarse fabrics. A tapestry needle has a blunt end and so is useful for lacing or whipping stitches, too.

Threads

Stranded cotton. This is a shiny, twisted thread. It has six strands which can be untwisted so as many or as few as liked can be used, depending on the embroidery being worked. It is suitable for most types of embroidery.

Pearl cotton is available in two thicknesses, No. 5 and No. 8. It is a smooth, corded thread used for all types of embroidery, but most often for counted-thread work.

Coton à broder is a very twisted, shiny thread, suitable for drawn-thread and drawn-fabric work and cutwork.

Soft embroidery thread is a thick, matt cotton used in most types of embroidery.

Tapestry wool is firm, twisted, woollen yarn, which can be used in ordinary embroidery as well as canvas work.
All the thread types, as listed above, are available in a good range of colours. In addition you may find it useful to have basting cotton, a range of mercerised cotton, some metal threads – gold and silver – in different thicknesses and to collect odds and ends of knitting yarns.
If you will want to wash your embroidery a lot, it is best to match yarn and fabric – cotton yarn on cotton fabric, for instance, and make sure your thread is colour fast. Always cut embroidery threads – never break them. Do not use too long a length at a time as it may fray. If it is a twisted thread, make sure it remains twisted during work.

Fabrics

Almost any fabric can be embroidered, but the stitches and design should be chosen to suit the material. Do not waste your efforts on embroidering a cheap fabric which will not last long.
For counted-thread work a fabric with an even weave must be used. Even-weave linen is inexpensive and is a very good choice for beginners, too, for either free-style or counted-thread work, as regular stitches can be made easily, right from the start.

Frames

All large embroideries should be worked in a frame, and so should most small ones, particularly if a delicate fabric is being used or if there are areas with a lot of stitches. There are two basic types of frame: the Swiss, or tambour, frame and the slate frame. The tambour frame consists of two loops, one slightly larger than the other. The fabric is placed over the smaller hoop, then the larger hoop is placed over the fabric so that it holds it taut. Some of these frames have a screw for tightening the outer hoop and some have a stand or clamp so the frame can be placed on a table. If a very fine fabric is being used, it is a good idea to have a piece of muslin or tissue between hoop and fabric.
The slate frame is rectangular and consists of two parallel horizontal bars. Each bar has a length of tape nailed along it. The fabric to be embroidered is sewn to the tape. The side pieces are then slotted into the bars and secured so that they hold the fabric taut. The fabric is laced to these side pieces with strong thread; if a very fine fabric is used, the sides of the fabric should first have strips of tape sewn to them and then the tape is laced to the side pieces of the frame.

Thimble

A metal one is preferable.

Scissors

You will need a large pair for cutting fabrics and a small pointed pair for cutting thread.

Also useful

In addition pins and pounce are needed to transfer designs (see page 54), a clean white cloth is needed for wrapping the embroidery in while it is not being worked, an iron, ironing board and pressing cloth will be required for pressing the work and a sewing machine is useful for finishing off a piece or making it up into its finished form.

TRANSFERRING

Purchased transfers

There are two types of embroidery transfers – single impression which are used once only, and multi-print which can be used up to eight times: the thinner the fabric the more often can the transfer be used. Cut any lettering away from the transfer and keep aside. Heat iron to fairly hot (wool) temperature for a single impression transfer or hot (cotton) temperature for a multi-print transfer. On a spare piece of fabric test the heat of the iron by placing the cut-away lettering face downwards on the fabric, running the iron over it for a few seconds, then peeling off the transfer. If a good impression has been

56

Worked in rows: bring needle out at bottom right edge of row. Insert 4 threads up and 4 threads to left and bring out again 4 threads down. Insert 4 threads up and 4 threads to left, then work this half of each cross all along row. On return journey work second arm of each cross to complete stitch.

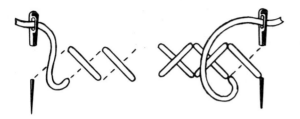

Feather stitch

Bring needle out at top of stitch line. Holding thread down with left thumb, insert needle a little to the right and bring out above thread a short distance down in the centre. Insert to the left and bring out above thread a little lower down (diagram 1). Double feather stitch has two stitches to the right and two to the left (diagram 2).

Fly stitch

Begin at top of stitch line and bring needle through a little to the left. Holding thread down with left thumb, insert needle an equal distance to the right of stitch line and bring out again on stitch line a short distance down. Make a short vertical stitch downwards, then bring needle out ready for next stitch. This stitch can be worked in rows or individually. When a single stitch is being made the vertical stitch is very tiny.

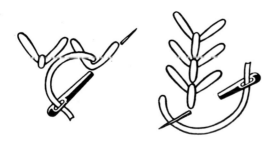

Opposite: *pink and white beach set (see page 37).*
Right: *motif waistcoat (see page 40).*

57

French knot

Bring needle through fabric and hold thread down with left thumb. Twist thread twice round needle. Still holding thread firmly turn needle and insert close to starting point. Pull tightly.

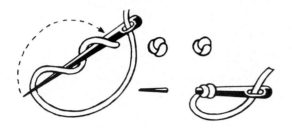

Herringbone stitch

Work from left to right. Bring needle out at bottom of area where stitching is to appear (diagram 1). Insert at top and to right, then take a small stitch to the left and then insert back at the bottom. Ideally the stitch taken up by the needle should be the same length as the space between stitches. If the stitches are worked close together they appear as two rows of back stitch on the reverse side of fabric – if wished, they can be worked in this way from the wrong side (diagram 2).

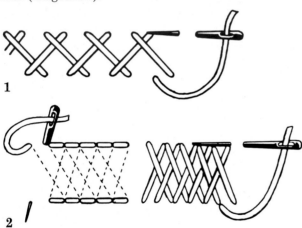

Holbein stitch or double running stitch

Work a row of running stitches (see above, right), with spaces between stitches the same length as the stitches themselves. Work a return

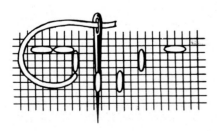

journey of running stitches, filling in the gaps left on the first row. This gives a continuous line of even stitches.

Overcast stitch

Work from left to right. Bring needle through just below stitch line and insert it just above. Bring it out again just below stitch line a little to the right. Continue in this way, following stitch line and working stitches close together.

Running stitch

Work from right to left. Bring needle through on stitch line and take it over 3 or 4 threads of the fabric then under 1 or 2 threads. Continue in this way, keeping all the same length, and all the spaces the same. This stitch can be threaded or laced, if wished.

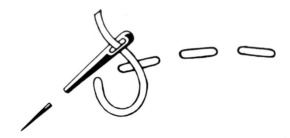

Satin stitch

Work straight stitches (see opposite) close together in space to be filled, bringing needle out for each new stitch only a thread of the fabric beyond previous stitch so you get a solid shape of stitching.

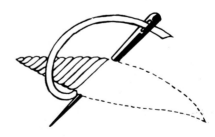

Opposite: *peasant-style blouse decorated with machine embroidery, in a variety of zigzag stitching.*

Stem stitch

Work from left to right. Bring needle out on stitch line then insert a little way along and slightly below line. Bring needle up a little way back just above stitch line. Continue in this way.

Straight stitch

Bring needle through as bottom of stitch area, insert at top then bring out at bottom of next stitch. Continue in this way. Straight stitches can be worked to form any shape or fill any area.

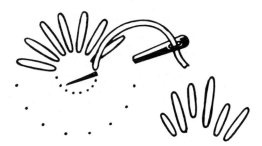

Above: *traditional floral embroidered pictures. Wild Rose (left) and Apple Blossom; Penelope Designs.*

Opposite: *floor-length curtains, with matching fabric valance, in a pretty floral print (see page 142).*

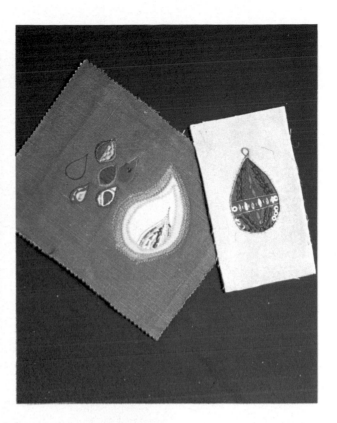

Above: '*White Landscape*', *a modern embroidery incorporating net, lace and beads.* **Right:** *machine embroidery samples.*

THE PATTERNS

Cushion and curtain holder

MATERIALS. Of Clark's Anchor Stranded Cotton (USA: J. & P. Coats Deluxe Six Strand Floss) — 9 skeins Coffee 0380, 6 skeins Flame 0334, 5 skeins Amber Gold 0309. ½ yd. white evenweave embroidery linen, 21 threads to 1 in., 59 in. wide. Piece of bonded fibre interfacing, 15¼ in. by 3 in. 2 curtains rings, each with a 1½-in. diameter. A cushion pad approx. 17 in. square. A Milward 'Gold Seal' tapestry needle No. 20.

STITCHES. Fly; back; satin; straight.

DIAGRAM. The diagram below gives a section of the design, showing the arrangement of the stitches on the threads of the fabric. The background lines on the diagram represent the threads of the fabric.

TO MAKE
Note. Use 6 strands of cotton throughout.
Cut 2 pieces, each 18 in. square, for cushion, and one piece 18 in. by 7 in. for curtain holder. Mark the centre thread of one large piece both ways with a line of basting stitches. The blank arrows on the diagram should coincide with your basting stitches.

Begin embroidery 8 threads down and 11 threads to the left of crossed basting stitches. Work the section given on the diagram, following stitch and colour key. Repeat section in reverse from black arrow to complete one side of lower left-hand square. Work other three sides to correspond, turning the corner as shown in the close-up photograph opposite. Work remaining three squares in a similar way.

Mark the centre of the curtain holder strip of fabric both ways with a line of basting stitches. These should coincide with the centre of bracket and curved arrow on the diagram. With long side facing, begin embroidery centrally and work section given on the diagram within the bracket.

To complete, repeat section ten times more to the right and to the left.

TO COMPLETE
Press embroidery on the wrong side. To make up cushion, place back and front fabric squares together, right sides facing, and machine stitch ½ in. from raw edges round three sides. Press seams and turn right side out. Insert cushion pad. Turn in seam allowance on remaining open edges and slipstitch neatly to close.

To make up curtain holder, trim fabric to within ½ in. of embroidery at each short end. Place interfacing centrally over embroidery on the wrong side and catchstitch in place. Fold curtain holder in half lengthwise, wrong side out, and sew long sides together ½ in. from raw edges. Turn to right side. Turn in ½ in. seam allowance on short ends and baste. Sew curtain rings in position to centre of embroidery at each short end then slipstitch openings closed.

STITCH AND COLOUR KEY
1   Amber gold Fly stitch
2   Flame Back stitch
3   Flame Satin stitch
4   Coffee Straight stitch

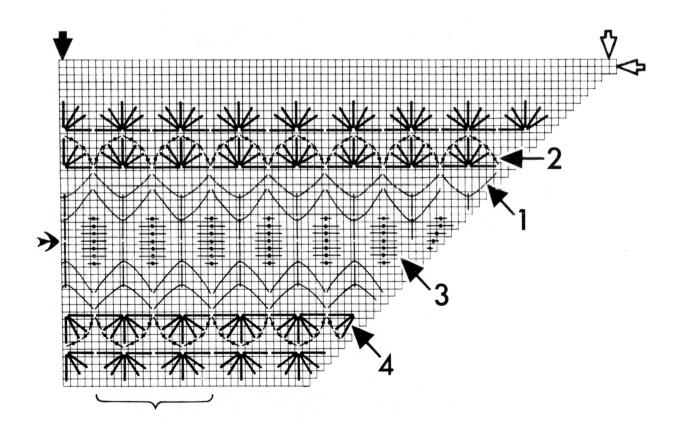

Beach Jacket
Illustrated in colour opposite

MATERIALS. Of Clark's Anchor Stranded Cotton (USA: J. & P. Coats Deluxe Six Strand Floss) — 3 skeins Peacock Blue 0170, 2 skeins each Periwinkle (dark) 0119, Parrot green 0253, 1 skein each Periwinkle (light) 0117 and (mid) 0118. A plain-coloured beach jacket, to match, tone or contrast with embroidery, with collar, cuffs and self-covered buttons. A Milward 'Gold Seal' crewel needle No. 7.

STITCHES. Satin; French knots; double knot

DIAGRAMS. Diagram A gives one motif in actual size.
Diagram B gives a guide to the stitches and thread colours used throughout the design.
Diagram C shows how to work double knot stitch: bring the thread through at A; take a small stitch across the line at B; pass the needle downwards under the surface stitch just made, without piercing the fabric, as at C. With the thread under the needle, pass the needle again under the first stitch at D. Pull the thread through to form a knot. The knots should be spaced evenly and closely to obtain a beaded effect.

TO MAKE
Note. Use 2 strands of cotton for double knot stitch; 3 strands for rest of embroidery.
With front of jacket facing, trace motif from diagram A on to lower left front 1½ in. from lower edge and 2 in. from centre front edge. Repeat motif twice more to the left seam, spacing evenly. Trace three motifs in reverse on to right front. With back of jacket facing, trace motif three times on to left half and then three times in reverse on to right half 1½ in. from lower edge. Trace motif centrally on to each cuff, and on to each side of collar.
Work embroidery following diagram B and stitch and colour key. All unnumbered parts on diagram B are worked in the same stitch and colour as the numbered parts most similar to them. Work a spiral of double knot stitches on to each covered button, as shown in photograph.

TO COMPLETE
Press embroidery on the wrong side.

STITCH AND COLOUR KEY
1 Light periwinkle Satin stitch
2 Mid periwinkle   Satin stitch
3 Dark periwinkle Satin stitch
4 Peacock blue   Satin stitch
5 Parrot green French knots
6 Peacock blue Double knot stitch

Diagram C

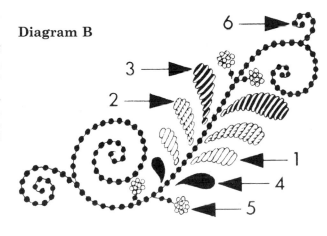

Diagram B

Diagram A

Embroidered beret

MATERIALS. Of Clark's Anchor Stranded Cotton (or Soft Embroidery, if preferred) (USA: J. & P. Coats Deluxe Six Strand Floss) — 5 skeins each Carmine Rose 041 and Terra Cotta 0338, 4 skeins Old Rose 075. ½ yd. fine woollen fabric, 45 in. wide. ½ yd. lining fabric, 36 in. wide. ½ yd. iron-on interfacing, 32 in. wide. ¾ yd. hat ribbon, 1½ in. wide. A Milward 'Gold Seal' chenille needle No. 19.

STITCHES. Stem; back; satin; fly; French knots.

DIAGRAMS. Diagram A (see page 68) gives the motif and outline for one panel of the beret in actual size.
Diagram B (below) gives a guide to the stitches and thread colours used throughout the design.

TO MAKE
Note. Use 6 strands of cotton throughout.
With one long side of woollen fabric facing, trace the motif as given in diagram A seven times along the fabric. The broken line indicates the cut edge, and the dotted line indicates the seam. Work embroidery, following diagram B and stitch and colour key. All unnumbered parts on diagram B are worked in the same stitch and colour as the numbered parts most similar to them.

TO COMPLETE
Press embroidery on the wrong side.
Iron interfacing on to wrong side of embroidered piece then cut sections along broken line. Machine stitch sides of sections, right sides together, along dotted lines. Trim seams to ¼ in.

To make top trimming cut a piece from woollen fabric, 12 in. by 2½ in. Turn back ½ in. on each long side and press. Roll fabric from one short end with the right side out. Turn in ½ in. on other short end and slipstitch to rolled piece. Stitch in position to centre of beret, as shown in photograph.
Cut seven sections from lining fabric, following broken line on diagram A. Join the sections together, right sides facing, stitching ⅛ in. in from dotted line, and trim. Place lining inside beret, wrong sides together, turn excess lining to wrong side and baste open edges together.
Stitch the ribbon to right side round edge. Join ribbon ends together, and press to inside of beret.

STITCH AND COLOUR KEY
1   Carmine rose Stem stitch
2   Terra cotta   Stem stitch
3   Old rose   Back stitch
4   Terra cotta Back stitch
5   Carmine rose Satin stitch
6   Carmine rose Fly stitch
7   Old rose French knots

Diagram B

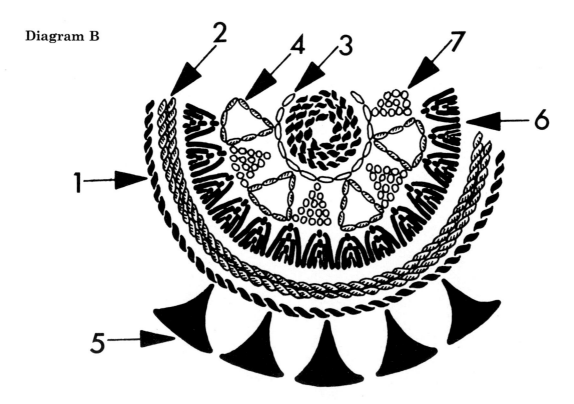

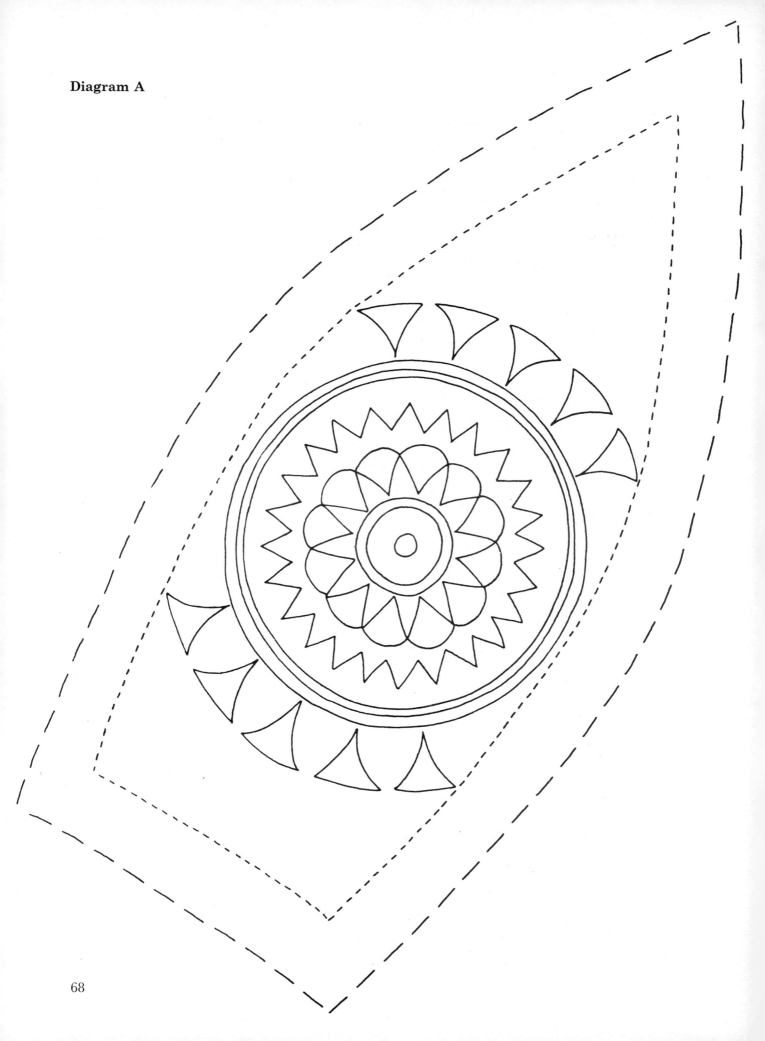

Flower motif workbag

MATERIALS. Of Coats Anchor Tapisserie Wool (or any good-quality tapestry wool) — 1 skein each Magenta 063, Apple Green 0279, Lemon 0288 and White 0402 (alternatively Clark's Anchor Stranded Cotton may be used, J. & P. Coats Deluxe Six Strand Floss in USA, using 6 strands of thread throughout). $\frac{5}{8}$ yd. mediumweight furnishing fabric, 48 in. wide. $\frac{5}{8}$ yd. lining fabric, 36 in. wide. 2 wooden handles, approx. 13 in. long, A Milward 'Gold Seal' chenille needle No. 19.

STITCHES. Stem; satin; detached chain; straight; French knots.

DIAGRAMS (see page 70). **Diagram A** gives one complete motif in actual size. **Diagram B** gives a guide to the stitches and thread colours used throughout the design.

TO MAKE

Cut one piece from furnishing fabric, 20 in. by 27 in. Fold fabric across the centre both ways and crease lightly. With one narrow side facing trace the motif as given in diagram A on to upper left-hand quarter 1½ in. from lengthwise fold and 2 in. from widthwise fold. Turn motif and repeat on upper right-hand quarter.

Work embroidery, following diagram B and stitch and colour key. All unnumbered parts on diagram B are worked in the same colour and stitch as the numbered parts most similar to them.

TO COMPLETE

Press embroidery on the wrong side.

Fold embroidered fabric in half widthwise, right sides together, and machine stitch down short sides leaving a 6-in. opening at the top. Turn to right side. Cut a piece from lining fabric, 20 in. by 24 in., and make up in a similar way leaving a 4½ in. opening.

Place lining inside bag, wrong sides facing. Turn in ½ in. seam allowance on top open edges and slipstitch neatly together. Attach handles by turning in 1 in. hems through slots in wooden handles and slipstitch in place taking care to include the edge of the lining.

STITCH AND COLOUR KEY
1   Lemon Stem stitch
2   Apple green Stem stitch
3   Lemon Satin stitch
4   Apple green Satin stitch
5   Apple green Detached chain stitch
6   Magenta Detached chain stitch
7   White Straight stitch
8   Magenta Straight stitch
9   White French knots

Diagram B

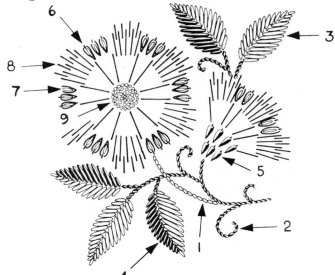

Diagram A

Cutwork cheval set

Illustrated on page 72

MATERIALS. Of Clark's Anchor Stranded Cotton (USA: J. & P. Coats Deluxe Six Strand Floss) — 3 skeins Peacock Blue 0170 and 2 skeins in White 0402. ½ yd. fine embroidery linen, 45 in. wide, in a colour to tone or contrast with embroidery colours. A Milward 'Gold Seal' crewel needle No. 6.

STITCHES. Stem; satin; buttonhole; French knots.

DIAGRAMS. Diagram A (page 73) gives one quarter of the design for the large mat in actual size; the double broken lines represent the shape of each small mat.
Diagram B (below) gives a guide to the stitches and thread colours used throughout the design.

TO MAKE

Note. Use 3 strands of cotton throughout.
Cut one piece from fabric, 11½ in. by 22 in., for large mat, and two pieces each 8 in. square for the small mats. Fold large piece across the centre both ways and crease lightly. Trace motif as given in diagram A on to lower left-hand quarter of fabric, omitting broken lines. The single broken lines should coincide with your centre folds. Trace motif in reverse on to upper left-hand quarter. To complete, turn fabric and repeat on opposite side.
Trace design as given centrally on to one small mat.
Trace in reverse on to other small mat.
Work embroidery, following diagram B and stitch and colour key. All unnumbered parts on diagram B are worked in the same stitch and colour as the numbered parts most similar to them.

TO COMPLETE

Press embroidery on the wrong side.
Cut away all parts of fabric marked with a cross on diagram A, and also surplus fabric round edges. Use small, sharp-pointed scissors, cutting from the wrong side and taking care not to snip the stitches.

STITCH AND COLOUR KEY

1 White Stem stitch
2 Peacock blue Stem stitch
3 White Satin stitch
4 White Buttonhole stitch
5 Peacock blue Buttonhole stitch
6 Peacock blue French knots

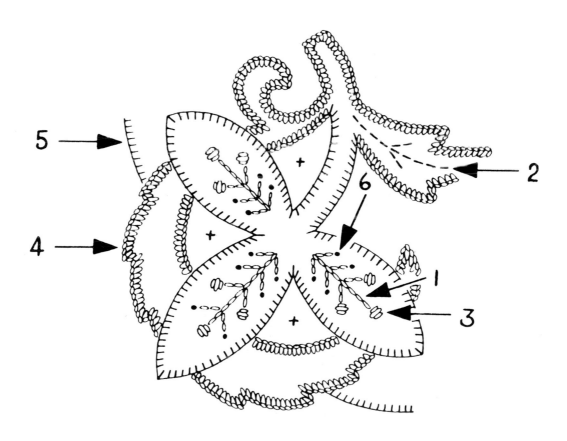

Diagram B

Cutwork cheval set – elegant for a dressing-table.
Instructions start on previous page.

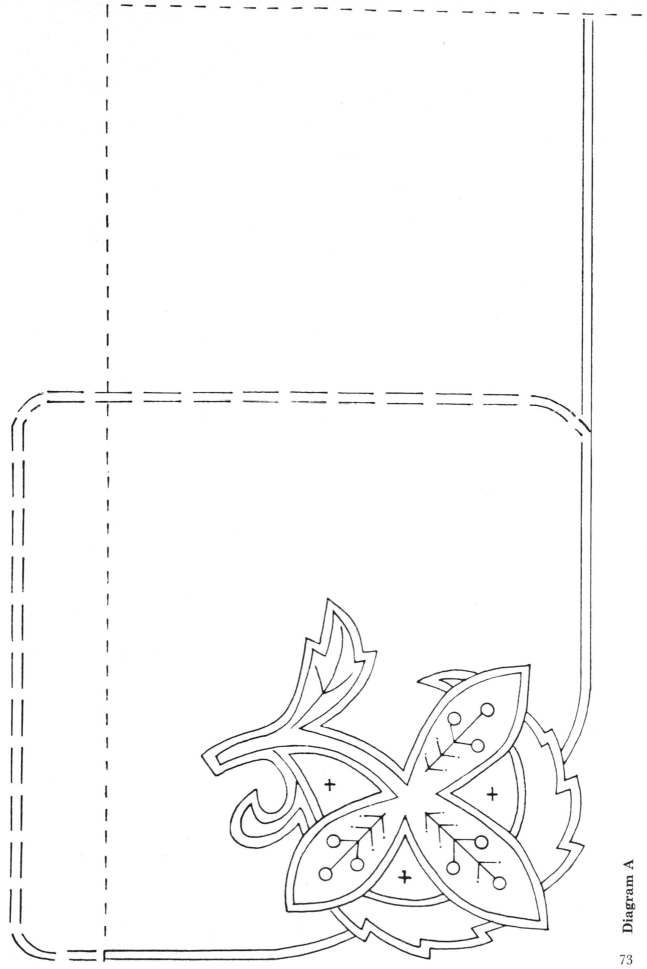

Diagram A

73

Girl's smocked dress

MATERIALS. Of Clark's Anchor Stranded Cotton (USA: J. & P. Coats Deluxe Six Strand Floss) — 1 skein each Cerise 033, Parrot Green 0253 and Gorse Yellow 0301. Pattern for a child's puff-sleeved dress suitable for smocking. Fine white fabric — amount quoted in the pattern. A Milward 'Gold Seal' crewel needle No. 6.

STITCHES. Wave; cable; surface honeycomb.

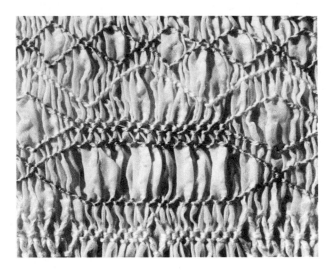

DIAGRAMS. Diagram A gives a guide to rows of gathers in actual size.

Diagram B (page 76) shows a section of smocking which is repeated across fabric. The dotted lines at the left-hand edge indicate the rows of gathers and show the placing of smocking stitches in relation to these rows. The broken vertical lines indicate the folds formed when the gathering threads are drawn up.

Diagram C indicates the position of rows of running stitches.

Diagram D shows how to work cable stitch: secure thread on first pleat on left-hand side. This stitch is worked over two pleats by catching up one pleat with the needle, the thread being alternately above and below the needle.

Diagram E shows how to work wave stitch: work from left to right, as in fig. 1. Begin with needle to the left of first pleat. Take stitch straight across first and second pleats, with thread below needle. Bring needle out to left of second pleat above stitch just made. Continue in this way until sixth pleat is reached. Have thread above needle for the stitch and bring needle out to left of sixth pleat, just below stitch. Work downward slope to correspond with upward. Fig. 2 shows the second row of wave stitches worked in reverse to form diamond pattern.

Diagram F shows how to work surface honeycomb stitch: bring the needle through on first pleat on lower level.

Draw the needle horizontally through the second pleat keeping the thread below the needle. With the thread still below, insert the needle horizontally through the same pleat on top level. With the thread above the needle, insert horizontally through third pleat on top level, and still with thread above, insert the needle through the same pleat on lower level. Continue in this way. Fig. 1 shows position of needle and thread when working stitch on top level; fig. 2 shows a second row of surface honeycomb stitch worked to form a diamond pattern.

Diagram A

Diagram C

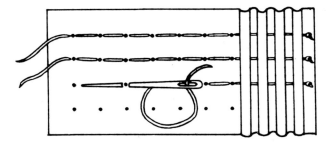

Diagram D

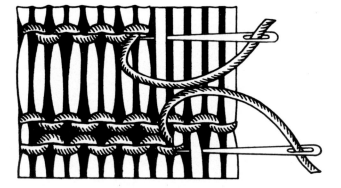

TO MAKE

Note. Use 3 strands of cotton throughout.

Cut out dress, using paper pattern. Trace the dotted section as given in diagram A on to wrong side of bodice front section, beginning ¾ in. in from top and side edges. Repeat section across width of fabric, the number of times required for the dress size you are making, ending ¾ in. from other side.

Now work running stitches across the dotted lines as in diagram C. Begin at right-hand side with a knot and back stitch to secure, and gather by picking up a small portion of the fabric on each dot. Use a new thread for each row, and leave ends loose. Draw up threads, easing gently to form pleats as shown, but do not pull too tightly. Tie loose ends firmly in pairs close to the last pleat.

Work smocking stitches, following diagram B and stitch and colour key.

TO COMPLETE

Place smocking on an ironing table wrong side up, and cover with a damp cloth. Pass a hot iron lightly over it — do not press. This sets the smocking.

Remove all gathering threads, and make up dress as instructed in the pattern.

STITCH AND COLOUR KEY

1 Gorse yellow Wave stitch
2 Parrot green Wave stitch
3 Cerise Wave stitch
4 Gorse yellow Cable stitch
5 Parrot green Cable stitch
6 Cerise Cable stitch
7 Gorse yellow Surface honeycomb stitch

Diagram E

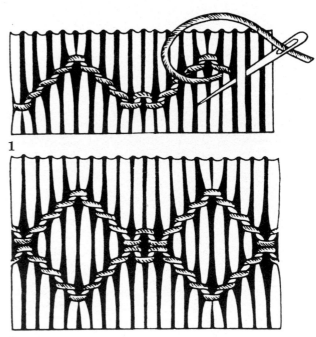

Diagram B

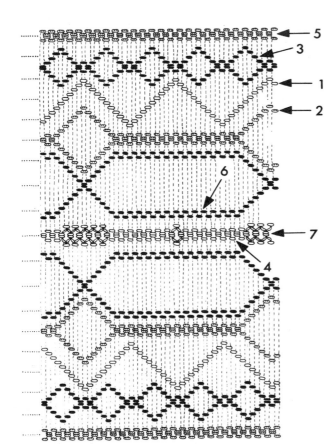

Diagram F

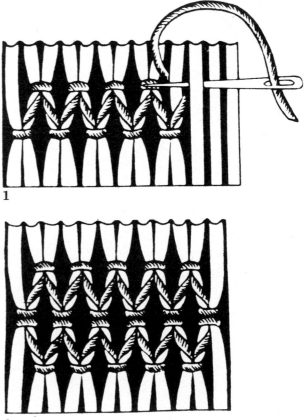

76

Chapter four
NEEDLEPOINT TAPESTRY

Needlepoint tapestry is, strictly speaking, not tapestry at all – for the word really means a woven fabric – but is embroidery on a canvas ground. When the embroidery is worked entirely in either tent or gobelin stitch, the effect thus achieved is similar to a woven tapestry, hence the name. But there is a great deal more to needlepoint besides these two traditional stitches; in fact there are dozens of interesting, attractive stitches which can be used, and once an understanding of the craft has been acquired it is possible to invent new stitches. Build up an extensive stitch vocabulary, learn to use threads and colours as an artist uses paints, and you will be able to create all manner of fascinating textures and effects.

EQUIPMENT

The basic equipment for needlepoint tapestry consists of thread, canvas and a frame.

Owl design bell pull, worked on a medium mesh, single-thread canvas, in a variety of different stitches.

Yarns

Traditionally, only linen, wool and silk threads are used for tapestry work, but in fact a wide range of threads, natural and synthetic, can be most effectively used depending on the type of design being worked. To begin with, however, stick to the conventional tapestry yarns: tapisserie wool (tapestry wool), crewel wool and stranded embroidery cottons. These are all good hard-wearing threads which will withstand the long and constant wear usually demanded by designs made up in needlepoint.

Embroidery cottons and crewel wool can be used in single or multiple strands to suit the canvas mesh; tapisserie wool can only be used in a single strand.

When you become experienced in needlepoint you will no doubt want to experiment with unusual and novelty threads. These can be most successfully used, but whichever yarn you choose to use should never be finer than the threads of the canvas or the background canvas will show through your stitches.

Canvas

Most designs made in needlepoint have to withstand fairly hard wear – for instance, church kneelers, handbags, chair seats, cushions. For this reason, it is important to buy a good-quality canvas. if you work your embroidery correctly, there should be no canvas visible after the design is complete, but nevertheless the choice of a good canvas will give your work a much longer life, and often help to show your stitches to best effect.

Canvas is usually made either from cotton or linen: which you choose is a matter of personal preference, although linen is probably the more hardwearing of the two.

Canvases are available in a choice of double thread or single. In double-thread canvasses, the warp and weft threads are arranged in pairs. For a beginner, a single-thread canvas is probably the best choice. Double-thread canvases can be used for detailed designs later where it is wished to use both tent stitch and trammed tent stitch in the same design.

Single and double-thread canvases are made in a range of mesh sizes, to suit different types of designs and different yarns. A wide mesh gives only a few threads or holes to the inch, and is useful for big-scale work; a fine mesh has considerably more threads or holes to the inch and should be used for intricate designs.

Canvases are sold by their mesh size: in a single-thread canvas this size is given as the number of threads to the inch; in double-thread canvas this is given by the number of holes to the inch. Mesh sizes usually range from about 10 to 30 threads or holes to the inch, but there are even bigger mesh canvases available, with only 4 or 5 holes to the inch, known as rug canvas.

Needles

The ideal tapestry needle should pass through the canvas easily, without forcing the threads of the canvas apart and without splitting the threads. Sizes of tapestry needles range from 13 through to 24. The lower the number the bigger the needle, so for fine intricate work you would choose a No. 24 needle.

Frames

Many of the stitches used in needlepoint tapestry are diagonal stitches, and if a frame is not used to stretch and control your canvas, then the canvas will be pulled out of shape by the continual slant of stitches in the same direction. There are a number of straight stitches in needlepoint and if you intend to work a design using only these stitches, then a frame will not be necessary.

A round embroidery frame is not suitable for needlepoint work: only use a square or rectangular frame. A simple frame can be easily made by stretching the canvas tautly and pinning it to a wooden picture frame. However there are a number of different types of ready-made frames available if you wish to buy one.

Leader frame. This is a simple rectangular frame which has to be supported at a comfortable working height in order to leave your hands free to stitch.

Table frame. A self-supported frame which can be placed on a table top. There are usually screw fittings to adjust the frame to give the slant required.

Floor frame. Probably the most versatile frame of all. A free-standing, adjustable frame, which can be placed anywhere with work left in position on it.

Travel frame. Not recommended for everyday use, but useful if you want to carry your work around, and for small pieces of work. The total depth of this frame is only 12 in., so your work has to be rolled up and re-rolled each time you need a fresh piece of canvas to work on.

Also useful

Scissors, tape measure, pins and drawing pins, blotting paper for stretching the canvas, waterproof Indian ink for transferring designs to your canvas.

FRAMING-UP CANVAS

Most frames operate on a similar principle: two horizontal, parallel rollers are covered with webbing to which your canvas is attached. The rollers then slot or screw into wooden side struts. The sides of your canvas are laced to these struts. The width of your canvas should never exceed the length of the webbing on the rollers of the frame.

Before fixing your canvas in position on the frame, you should cut your canvas to size – this should be the size of finished embroidery plus at least 3 in. extra all round. Mark the centre points horizontally and vertically on your canvas with lines of basting stitches. Make ½ in. turnings at top and bottom edges of canvas, and baste in place. Enclose these and the side edges with a length of 1–in. tape. Now position canvas on your frame, and stitch top edge of canvas with overcasting stitches to top roller, bottom edge to bottom roller. Finally lace side edges of canvas to side struts of frame, using string or strong button thread. The lacing should be taken through the taped edge of canvas and then round the strut of frame, at regular intervals.

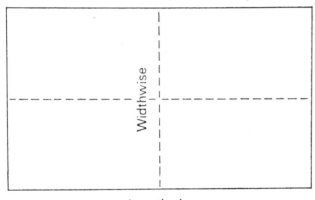

Lengthwise

STITCHES
Brick stitch

This stitch is worked in rows alternately from the left and from the right. It is usually worked over 4 horizontal threads of the canvas, between alternate pairs of vertical threads. Bring needle through at lower point of each stitch and work

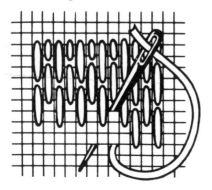

stitch upwards. In the following row, stitches are worked in the spaces between stitches of previous row to give an interlocked 'brick' formation.

Cross stitch

See page 55.

Double cross stitch

A variation on the basic cross stitch. Work a basic cross over 4 horizontal and 4 vertical threads. Bring needle out 4 threads down and 2 vertical threads to the left. Insert needle 4 threads up and bring out 2 threads to the left and 2 horizontal threads down. Complete stitch by inserting needle 4 threads to the right and bring out 2 threads down and 4 threads to the left in readiness for the next stitch.

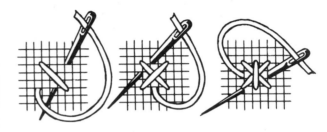

Fern stitch

Work from top to bottom. Bring needle through at top left-hand corner and take a diagonal stitch 2 vertical threads to the right and 2 horizontal threads down. Bring needle through 1 vertical thread to the left. Insert 2 vertical threads to the right, 2 horizontal threads up. Bring back out 3 threads to the left, 1 thread down. Continue in this way.

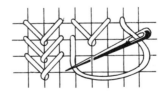

Opposite: *the fabric and style of your curtains should be chosen with care so they complement and blend with the decor of your home. See chapter on Making Soft Furnishings, starting on page 134.*

Flat stitch

This is worked in blocks of diagonal stitches, each block consisting of 3 stitches and covering 2 horizontal threads and 2 vertical threads. Blocks of stitches slant alternately to the left and to the right.

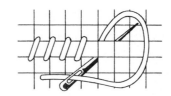

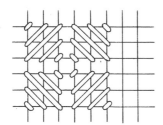

Florentine stitch

This stitch is usually worked in rows of different colours, to form an allover wave pattern. Stitches are straight and vertical, and can be worked over any number of canvas threads. They are 'stepped' as shown in the diagram, below, and the size of the step may also be varied. A common version of the stitch is to work each vertical stitch over 4 horizontal threads, stepping each stitch up or down 2 threads at a time. Each row is an exact repetition of the previous one, so stitches fit together.

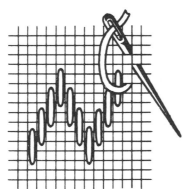

Gobelin stitch

Work in rows alternately from the left and from the right. In the first row, worked from left to right, work diagonal stitches across 1 vertical thread to the left and 2 horizontal threads down. Bring needle out 2 horizontal threads up and 2 vertical threads to the right. In the following row, needle is inserted from above downwards instead of upwards from below to give the same slant of stitch.

Half cross stitch

This is simply the first half of the complete basic cross stitch. It may be worked from left to right, or right to left.

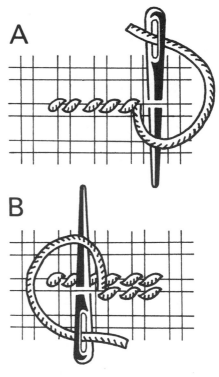

Hungarian stitch

This is worked in groups of 3 vertical stitches, each worked in turn over 2, 4 and 2 horizontal threads; 2 vertical threads are left between each group, so stitches in the following row can be worked to give an interlocked pattern.

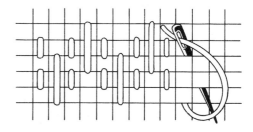

Knotted stitch

Work a diagonal stitch over 3 horizontal and 1 vertical threads, then work a small horizontal stitch over the centre of the diagonal stitch to tie it down. Work in rows, overlapping each row by 1 thread of the canvas.

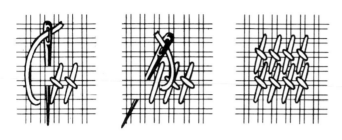

Long-legged cross stitch

Another variation on the basic cross stitch. Long-legged cross stitch is worked from left to right and one of the crossing stitches is worked over double the number of threads of the other stitch. Diagram A shows the method of working the stitch. Diagram B shows three stitches completed.

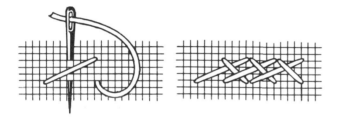

Rice stitch

In this a basic cross stitch is worked over 4 horizontal and 4 vertical threads, then a small straight stitch is worked over each corner of the basic cross. It is usual to work the crossed corner stitches in a contrasting yarn and colour to the basic cross.

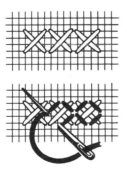

Satin stitch

This is a simple straight stitch, which may be horizontal or vertical, worked from right to left, or left to right, and over any number of threads as required.

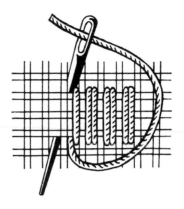

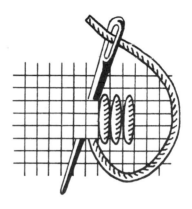

Scottish stitch

Blocks of 5 diagonal stitches covering 3 horizontal and 3 vertical threads of the canvas, are outlined with tent stitches, each worked over a single intersection of canvas threads.

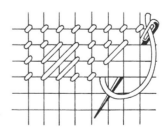

Tent stitch

Sometimes known as petit point stitch. It may be worked over single canvas, or if worked over double-thread canvas then the threads are

Diagram B

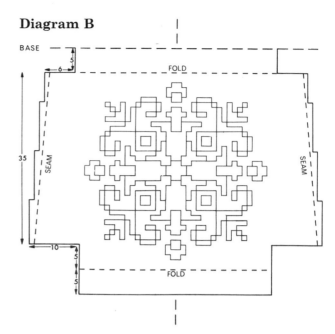

Diagram A

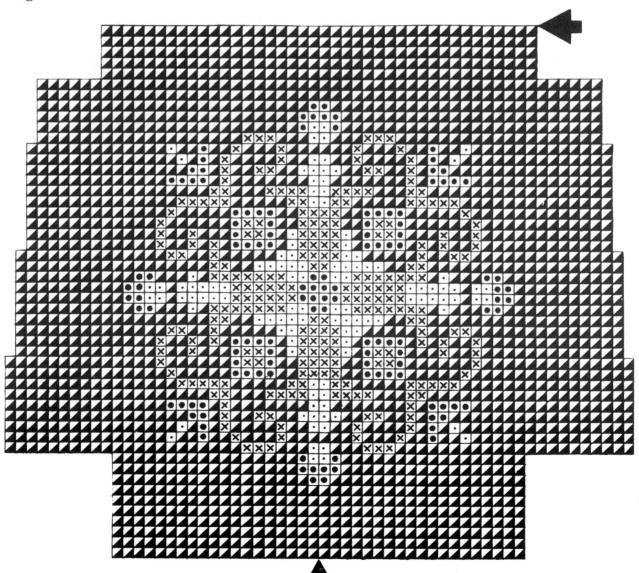

Geometric cushion
Illustrated in colour on page 89

MATERIALS. Of Coats Anchor Tapisserie wool (or any good-quality tapestry wool) — 8 skeins Petunia 063, 6 skeins Mid Violet 097, 5 skeins Dark Muscat Green 0844, 4 skeins Dark Violet 0417, and 2 skeins Pale Muscat Green 0842. ⅝ yd. single-thread tapestry canvas, 18 threads to 1 in., 23 in. wide. ⅝ yd. furnishing satin or similar mediumweight furnishing fabric, 48 in. wide, for backing, in a colour to match, tone or contrast with the embroidery. A Milward 'Gold Seal' tapestry needle No. 19. Cushion pad approximately 16½ in. square.

MEASUREMENTS. Finished cushion measures approximately 16½ in. square.

DIAGRAM. The diagram below gives the complete design. Each background square on the diagram represents one block of 4 satin stitches worked over 4 threads of the canvas.

TO MAKE
Mark the centre of canvas both ways with a line of basting stitches. Prepare canvas, and frame-up.
Begin embroidery centrally, following diagram and colour key. The arrows on the diagram should coincide with your basting stitches. The design is worked throughout in blocks of 4 satin stitches, each stitch worked over 4 threads of the canvas.

TO COMPLETE
Trim canvas to within 1 in. of embroidery. Cut a piece the same size from backing fabric. Place back and front pieces right sides together and sew close to the embroidery, leaving an opening on one side so that the pad may be inserted easily. Turn to right side. Insert cushion pad. Turn in the seam allowance on the open edges and slipstitch neatly together.

COLOUR KEY

⊡	Petunia
☒	Mid violet
■	Dark violet
☐	Pale muscat green
◪	Dark muscat green

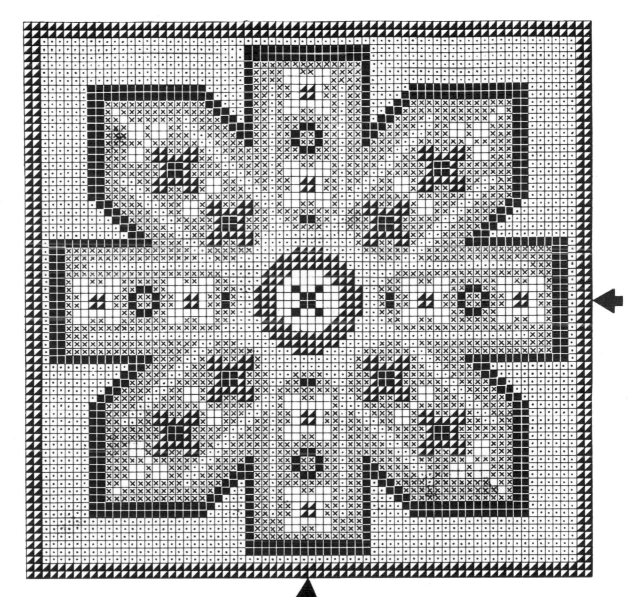

Florentine handbag and spectacle case

Illustrated in colour on page 92

MATERIALS, Of Clarks Anchor Tapisserie Wool (or any good-quality tapestry wool) — 8 skeins Mid Muscat Green 0843, 6 skeins Dark Muscat Green 0845, 5 skeins Light Muscat Green 0842, 4 skeins Light Apple Green 0278, 3 skeins Mid Mustard 0309, 2 skeins each Lemon Yellow 0288 and Light Mustard 0308, 1 skein Buttercup 0306. $\frac{3}{4}$ yd. single-thread tapestry canvas, 18 threads to 1 in., 23 in. wide. $\frac{1}{2}$ yd. interfacing, 32 in. wide. $\frac{1}{2}$ yd. lining fabric, 36 in. wide. 8$\frac{1}{2}$-in. handbag frame, with detachable rods. A piece of cardboard 3 in. by 10 in. A Milward 'Gold Seal' tapestry needle No. 19.

MEASUREMENTS. Finished size of handbag is 10 in. high, 10 in. wide, 3 in. deep at base. Spectacle case: 2$\frac{1}{2}$ in. by 6 in.

DIAGRAMS. Diagram A gives a section of the complete design. The background lines on the diagram represent the threads of the canvas.
Diagram B gives one half of the design for the handbag, indicating how motifs are repeated across work. The numbers indicate the threads of the canvas. The broken line within the diagram indicates the amount to be worked for the spectacle case.

TO MAKE

Mark the centre of canvas widthwise with basting stitches. Mark the canvas lengthwise 8 in. from right-hand side, to allow for working the spectacle case on the left-hand side of the canvas.
Prepare canvas, and frame-up.
Begin embroidery for handbag centrally at crossed basting stitches and work section given in diagram A. The design is worked throughout in Florentine stitches, each stitch taken across 6 threads of the canvas as indicated on diagram A. The white arrows should coincide with your basting stitches. Follow colour key as a guide to threads.
Work the horizontal stitches last.
Complete one half of the embroidery, following diagram B for position of motifs. Work other half to correspond.
For spectacle case, work section within broken line on diagram B twice on remaining canvas.

TO COMPLETE

Handbag. Trim canvas to within 1 in. from embroidery on all sides. Using this as a pattern cut one piece each from interfacing and lining. Fold embroidered piece in half, wrong side out, and stitch side seams close to embroidery. Fold, so that side seam lies centrally along base section and stitch across base sides. Turn to right side. Make up interfacing and lining in a similar way. Lightly herringbone stitch cardboard in position to interfacing to form base. Insert in bag; turn down seam allowance of canvas on gusset edges over interfacing and stitch lightly. Turn in sides of section to go over rods, then fold in half and secure in place to interfacing along edge of embroidery. Insert lining in bag, turn down seam allowance level with gusset edges on all sides and slipstitch. Insert rods.
Spectacle case. Trim canvas to within $\frac{3}{4}$ in. from embroidery on all sides. Cut lining the same size. Place back and front pieces right sides together and stitch close to the embroidery, leaving top edges and 1$\frac{1}{4}$ in. down from sides for opening. Turn to right side. Make up lining in a similar way and insert in case. Turn in seam allowance on open edges and slipstitch lining to case.

94

COLOUR KEY

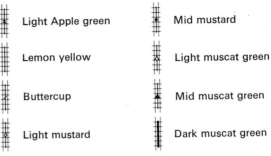

Light Apple green	Mid mustard
Lemon yellow	Light muscat green
Buttercup	Mid muscat green
Light mustard	Dark muscat green

Diagram A

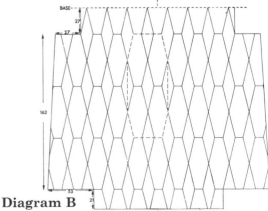

Diagram B

Chapter five
MACRAMÉ

Macramé is one of the newest old crafts to be revived in recent years. The basis of the craft is simply tying knots in lengths of string, rope, cord or other yarn, and by arranging knots in a decorative pattern to build up a fabric – fashion accessories, belts, bags, jewellery and dress trimmings, can be quickly and effectively made in this way, and also decorations for the home – wall hangings, cushion covers, lampshades, tablecloths, curtains, No hooks, tools, needles or other implements are necessary, so within minutes of learning to tie the two basic knots it is possible for even a child to make a simple belt, or a bag. Once a complete knowledge of knotting techniques has been acquired, and an understanding of the permutations of the basic knots, there is virtually no limit to the designs it is possible to create – just by tying knots.

Chains of flat knots worked in assorted yarns, strings and cords.

EQUIPMENT

Of all crafts, macramé requires the absolute minimum of equipment: all that is needed is a ball of string, a pair of scissors – and your hands. There are however various other 'aids' which will help your work along.

Yarns

Traditionally macramé has always been worked in string, or a strong linen thread, and this type of 'hard' yarn certainly gives the most satisfactory results. However it is possible to produce attractive fashion garments, for instance, using ordinary knitting yarns, in natural or synthetic fibres. Rug wool is particularly good, as it is more 'stable' than some of the finer knitting wools. Also because it is thick, knotting grows quickly. Any type of cotton yarn works well, especially piping cord, and all forms of cords, natural or synthetic. The 'harder' the yarn, the crisper will be the finished knotted fabric. Novelty yarns, such as Goldfingering, mixtures, metal threads and other similar, special-effect yarns, can also be effectively used. It is worth spending time browsing round shops and stores which sell all sorts of yarns – marine stores, for instance, often yield fascinating treasures – so do hardware departments, gardening stores, art and craft shops, and even theatrical supply stores. Part of the enjoyment of macramé work is seeking out and discovering new materials.

Pins

These are essential to control your work and to anchor it to a working surface. Ideally, use 'T' pins, or the rustless, glass-headed variety.

Working surface

Although it is possible to knot small pieces of work on your knee, you will find working a great deal more comfortable if you anchor your knotting to a rigid surface. For flat pieces of work, a working board can be easily made from a piece of soft wood (any wood which will easily take pins), or a hard wood padded with foam plastic or towelling. Cork makes a good working surface. A tape measure glued across the top and down one side edge of your board gives a useful, at-a-glance guide to measurements, and if you also rule out your surface into 1-in. squares this will help you keep the lines of your design straight and regular.

If you are working 'in the round', then a three-dimensional working base should be used – ideally this should be as near to the finished shape and size of the design you are making as possible as shaping will be achieved by easing knots over the surface. Cut a block of wood to the approximate size and shape required, and then pad it with foam plastic or towelling. If you are making a hat, then a wig stand gives an excellent working base.

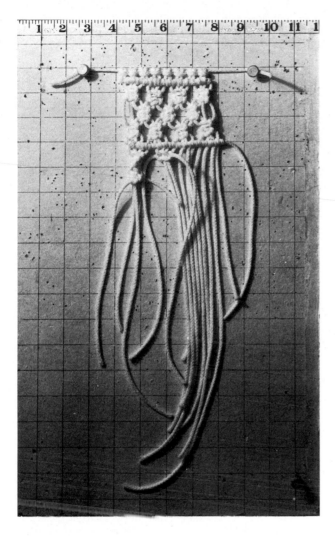

mid-knotting should one length fall short. For this reason yarn has to be cut into lengths long enough to take you right through your chosen pattern. Estimating what length this should be is not always easy, as some knotting patterns use up more cord than others. As a very approximate guide however, a reasonable estimate is to cut each cord length to eight times the length you want the finished design to be. If a fringe is wanted, this measurement should then be added. For example, if you wish to make a bag to measure 12 in. deep, with a plain (unknotted) fringe of 4 in., then cords should be cut to 8 ft. 4 in. (eight times twelve, plus four). This method applies when cords are 'set on' (see below) doubled to give two working cords (the usual method). Occasionally however a pattern may instruct you to set on cords singly – in this case they need only be cut to four times the finished length required.

As you become familiar with knotting patterns and techniques you will be able to assess which knots use up a lot of cord, and which use only a little, and cut your cords accordingly. Naturally one does not wish to waste expensive yarn unnecessarily, but in the early stages it is advisable to over-estimate your needs rather than risk running short and so spoiling an attractive design.

If you have to cut a large number of cords for a particular design, it is worth measuring out the length you will be cutting against a table edge or similar surface, and marking this area. It is then a simple matter to measure out your cord lengths against the markers. To keep cords orderly and prevent tangling, group cords as you cut them into batches of ten each and tie them loosely together. This will also help to keep count of the number of cords you have cut.

Also useful

A selection of beads, buttons and other oddments which can be incorporated in your knotting, glue and transparent self-adhesive tape for securing cord ends, drawing pins, tape measure, needle and sewing thread for making up items, or stitching cord ends to back of work.

STARTING WORK

Measuring and cutting cords

Probably the most tedious part of macramé work is the initial preparation required, before you can begin the exciting business of knotting. Contrary to most other crafts where you can launch almost straight away into creative work, and attend to making-up and neatening details afterwards, with macramé almost all the 'ground work' must be carried out at the beginning. If the details are carefully and accurately attended to first, then knotting should proceed easily and smoothly through to the finished design.

It is, for instance, difficult – and sometimes even impossible – to join on a new length of cord in

Setting on cords

With your cords cut to size the next step is to mount them ready for knotting to begin. This process is usually referred to as 'setting on', and cords may be either set on to another length of yarn (known as a **holding cord**), or they may be set on to a metal or wooden bar or ring (for instance for a wall hanging), or on to the bar of a buckle for a belt.

To set on to a holding cord, cut a length of yarn the width of your design plus 6 in. Tie a knot near one end by taking the string over and round itself, and through the loop formed. Pull knot tight. This is an **overhand knot**. Tie a similar knot near the other end of the cord, then pin the

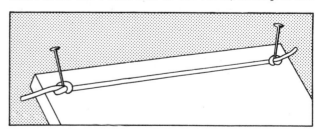

cord to your working surface, near the top, and stretching the cord as tautly as possible. Insert pins through the overhand knots.

Now you are ready to set on your cut cords: to do this, take each cord in turn, double it and insert the looped end under the holding cord from top to bottom. Take the loose ends of the doubled cord, pull them over the holding cord and down through the loop. Draw tight. Repeat with every cord until all are set on to the holding

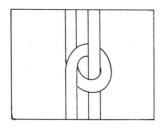

cord. Position each doubled set-on cord close to the previous one. Each individual cord length is now referred to as a knotting or working cord – there should be double the number of knotting cords, as the number of cords you cut. For instance, if you cut ten cords, now they are set on you will have twenty working or knotting cords.

THE KNOTS

Half hitch

This may be worked from the left or from the right. In its simplest form, you need only 2 knotting cords. To work the knot from the left, hold cord 2 taut, and take cord 1 across cord 2, then under it from right to left, and down through the loop formed. Draw tight, this is one half hitch (A). Continue to repeat the knot to form a chain. As cord 1 forms the knot, it is known as a **knotting cord**; cord 2 is the **knotbearing cord.**

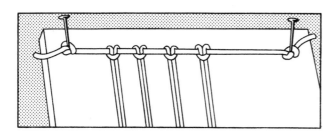

A   B

To tie a half hitch from the right, the procedure is reversed. Cord 1 becomes the knotbearing cord and it is held taut, while cord 2 is the knotting cord and is taken across cord 1, then up under it from left to right and down through loop (diagram B).

Reversed double half hitch

This knot can be used to create attractive braids. It consists of one half hitch worked in the normal way followed by a half hitch worked in reverse – i.e. take knotting cord under the knotbearing cord, round and over it and through the loop formed. A reversed double half hitch may be worked from the left or from the right.

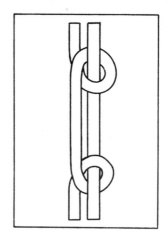

Flat knot

This knot is the basis for most macramé fabrics, or if the knot is worked in a continuous chain the result is a strong, hardwearing braid which can be used for a handbag handle, for a belt, or even for a dog lead. In its simplest form, a minimum of 4 cords are needed. In this case 2 cords (the 2 outside ones) are knotting cords; the 2 centre cords are knotbearers. It is important at all times that the centre knotbearing cords are kept as taut as possible, as this is the secret of tying an even, regularly-shaped flat knot. The knot is tied in 2 stages: begin by taking cord 1 under cords 2 and 3 and over cord 4. Now bring cord 4 over 2 and 3 and under 1. Pull gently into place. This is the first stage of the knot, and is known as the **half knot.**

Complete the flat knot by bringing cord 1 back under cords 3 and 2 and over 4. Bring cord 4 over 2 and 3 and under 1. Pull gently into place below first half knot.

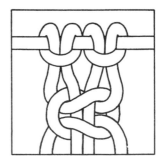

Multiend flat knot

This is merely a flat knot worked with multiple thicknesses of string. It can be worked with single knotting cords as in the basic flat knot, and all the extra cords used to give a multiple knotbearing centre; or cords may be divided evenly to give multiple knotting cords, and multiple knotbearing cords; or you may have only 2 knotbearing centre cords as in the basic knot, and the remaining cords divided evenly to give 2 equal groups of multiple knotting cords.

Cording

This is an important macramé technique. It can be worked horizontally, vertically or diagonally, and used to shape edges, to create solid fabrics or open-work lacy patterns, and once the technique has been fully mastered it can also be used to 'draw' figures. A row of horizontal cording worked immediately after cords have been set on gives a good firm start to knotting, and similarly a row of horizontal cording can be worked at the end of a design to bring it to a neat conclusion. In a design which used different panels of pattern a dividing row of cording between each panel introduces a pleasing element of order (see sampler wall hanging, page 101). Cording is based on the half hitch, and each complete knot in cording, whether it is worked horizontally, vertically or diagonally, consists of two half hitches worked closely together. The complete knot is known as a double half hitch.

Horizontal cording

The knotbearing cord in cording is called a **leader cord** and this may be either one of the set-on cords or it may be a separate cord. To work cording with a separate leader, cut a new cord similar in length to each of your set-on cords. Tie an overhand knot near one end of the leader cord and pin it through the knot to your working surface, positioning it just below holding cord edge and to the left of the first set-on cord. Stretch leader tautly across working cords, then beginning with set-on cord on far left,

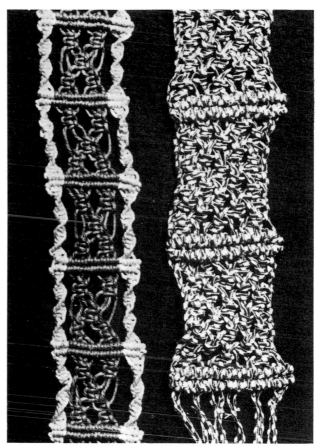

Two braids – flat knot patterns separated by rows of cording.

To work a second row of horizontal cording immediately below the first, place a pin in your working surface to the right of the last knot in the first row, then bring leader round the pin and stretch it tautly across work as before, but this time from right to left. Work double half

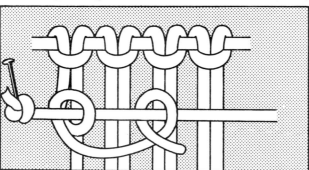

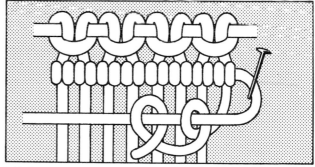

bring it up in front of leader, then down behind it and bring end through to the left of loop formed round leader. Repeat this process exactly: this completes one double half hitch. Continue in this way along row of set-on cords, tying a double half hitch with each cord in turn round leader. Draw each knot tightly and push it close to the previous one.

hitches across row over leader, working this time from right to left. Now each half hitch will be tied by bringing working cord up and over leader, then down behind it and the end brought through to the right of the loop formed.

Diagonal cording

This is worked in a similar way to horizontal cording, but leader cord is placed across work at an angle, according to where you wish the line of cording to appear.

Pins

Use good-quality steel pins, as these will not leave rust marks or holes in your fabric.

Scissors

Three pairs are required: shears for cutting fabrics, a medium sized sharp pair for cutting paper, and a small pointed pair for clipping seams. Pinking shears are also useful.

Sewing threads

Again a varied selection is best. For general use, a 60 cotton or 50 or 60 mercerised cotton (ordinary mercerised) is best. For heavy fabrics, such as tweed or corduroy, use a 40 cotton or 40 mercerised cotton (heavy duty mercerised). For fine and sheer fabrics, use a fine nylon or Terylene thread, or a fine mercerised. There are good-quality multi-purpose threads also available which can be used with all fabric types and weights.

Also useful

Tape measure; yard stick; iron; ironing board and sleeve board; pressing cloth; tailor's chalk; dressmaker's carbon paper and tracing wheel; thimble; hem marker; stitch unpicker; paper and pencil.

FABRICS

If you already make your own clothes you will know how exciting fabric shops and departments can be! In fact the selection of a suitable fabric can sometimes be difficult because there is such a wonderful range of designs and fabric types to choose from. However, if you are a beginner, then it is best to limit your choice to an easy-to-handle fabric. Slippery materials and ones that fray easily can try the patience of the most experienced dressmaker. Cotton fabrics are good for beginners; so are the cotton and wool mixtures, and fine wools.

A plain fabric which will not need lining is a good choice. If you choose a pattern, then make sure it is a small irregular one. Checks, stripes and prints with a large or regular pattern repeat are tricky, as they need careful matching at seams and edges. The fabric chart below will serve as a guide to the basic fabrics generally available, and any special treatment these fabrics require.

Fabric Guide

Fabric	Description	Thread, Needle & Tension	Pressing	Special Care
Brocade	Heavy fabric, with raised patterns. Made from silk, cotton or synthetics.	Ordinary mercerised cotton or silk; medium machine needle; 12–14 sts. per in.	Moderate iron.	Neaten seams to prevent fraying.
Cotton	A natural fibre, available in different patterns and weights.	Lightweight fabrics: ordinary mercerised cotton; fine machine needle; 16–20 sts. per in. Heavy fabrics: medium machine needle; 12–14 sts. per in.	Hot iron.	Starch lightly for a crisp finish.
Corduroy	Cotton pile fabric in narrow or wide ribs.	Heavy-duty mercerised cotton; medium-coarse needle; 10–12 sts. per in.	As for velvet.	Cut pattern with pile of fabric running up.
Linen	A natural fabric. Light or heavy weight.	As for cotton.	A hot iron over a damp cotton cloth.	—
Silk	Various types available — e.g. tussah, shantung, tulle.	Sheers: fine machine needle; 16–20 sts. per in. Heavier weights: same needle; 8–10 sts. per in. Use silk thread.	Moderate iron.	—
Synthetics	Various types usually sold under trade names — Dacron, Courtelle, Crimplene, Tricel etc. All strong, hard-wearing man-made fabrics.	Terylene, nylon or multi-purpose thread; fine machine needle. Fine fabrics: 15–20 sts. per in. Heavier fabrics: 10–12 sts. per in.	Cool iron, if pressing is necessary.	Do not spin dry.
Velvet	Pile fabric made from cotton, nylon, silk or rayon.	Heavy-duty mercerised cotton for cotton, silk or wool; nylon or Terylene for synthetics; medium needle; 10–12 sts. per in.	Use a velvet pressing board or stand dry iron upright. Place a damp cloth over wrong side of fabric, pass back and forth over iron.	Cut pattern with pile of fabric running up and baste seams before sewing to prevent slipping.
Wool	Many different types and weights, from fine light-weight qualities for dresses to heavy qualities for coats.	Light and medium weights: ordinary mercerised cotton, medium needle; 12–14 sts. per in. Heavy weights: medium-coarse needle; 10–12 sts. per in.; heavy-duty mercerised cotton.	Warm iron over a damp wool cloth.	Place strips of paper between seam and dress when pressing to stop seams showing through.

YOUR SEWING MACHINE

It is worth spending time getting to know your sewing machine. Study the instruction book which is usually supplied with a machine and learn exactly what your machine is capable of doing. The instruction book should also tell you how to thread the machine, fit the needle and alter the tension or length of stitch to suit different fabrics. As a general rule, the finer the fabric the shorter the stitches should be. Heavy, thicker fabrics need longer stitches.

If you have never used a sewing machine before, have several practice sessions on odd scraps of material before you embark on making a finished garment. Begin by sewing straight lines of stitches. Use a soft pencil to draw lines on your fabric scraps then stitch along these guide lines. Then try square, zigzags and curved lines, working at different speeds. Then do the same exercises without pencil guide lines.

Once you are proficient on one layer of fabric, do the same stitches on two layers, pinning the layers together with the pins at right angles to the line of machining, and stitching $\frac{1}{2}$ in. from edge of fabric. If your machine has a hinged foot you can machine over the pins, but with a fixed or rigid foot you must take them out as they reach the presser foot otherwise you could damage the needle.

It is always a good idea before making up any garment to take two scraps of the fabric you are using, pin them together and machine a few lines — curved, straight and zigzag. Look carefully at the fabric and see if it has puckered, on one or both sides. If both sides are puckered, the tension is too tight and the stitch probably too small. Loosen the tension, lengthen the stitch (i.e. a lower number of stitches per inch) and try again. If only the under layer is puckered your fabric is 'travelling'. It must be basted before you machine any seams; otherwise, without basting, the under layer will always end up shorter.

BASIC TECHNIQUES

Note. Other important sewing techniques, such as putting in a zip, making pockets, and lining a garment, are included in the patterns to make, starting on page 114.

Seam finishes

If you intend to line a garment, then it is not necessary to finish the seams. Merely press the seams open before stitching lining in place. All unlined garments should have their seams finished by any of the following methods. Neatening seams prevents unravelling of fabrics which are inclined to fray easily, and also strengthens the seam and gives a 'professional' look to your finished garment.

Pinking. This is one of the easiest and quickest methods of all seam finishes, and is ideal for inexpensive, closely woven fabrics such as cotton. All you have to do is to cut along seam edges with pinking shears.

Machine stitching. This is a good strong finish for thinner fabrics like fine wool, linen, light-weight cotton and synthetics. Turn under raw edge for about $\frac{1}{4}$ in. and machine stitch close to fold.

Zigzag edging. If you have a swing needle or zigzag attachment on your machine, all fabrics can be neatened in this way. Just stitch along edges of turnings, adjusting width of zigzag and length of stitch to suit fabric. A loosely woven material needs a deep zigzag, a finer fabric can take a smaller, narrower one.

Bound edges. Excellent for loosely woven tweeds or unlined jackets. Take a 1 in. wide bias strip of fine linen or silk to match fabric, and stitch, right sides together, to the raw seam edges about $\frac{1}{4}$ in. from edge. Fold the strip over raw edge and machine stitch again along seam, close to fold.

Oversewing. This is the only method of seam finishing which should be left until garment is complete. Trim the seams neatly, cutting away any loose threads, and then work small slanting stitches by hand over the raw edges. Work from left to right.

French seam. This seam should be used for all sheer and very fine fabrics. With wrong sides of fabric together baste along seam line. Stitch $\frac{1}{4}$ in. above basting. Trim seam close to stitching, remove basting, press seam to one side. Turn seam to inside so right sides of fabric are together. Stitch along seamline, press and open. First seam should have been trimmed enough to prevent any raw edges showing.

Layering and clipping turnings

The seam allowance on the curved edges on any part of a garment should always be layered and clipped so they will lie flat and even, with no unsightly bumps.

Layering. When two or more layers of fabric are seamed and pressed together — round a collar edge, neckline or armhole — the turnings should be 'layered'. This means each turning should be trimmed (after seam has been stitched) slightly narrower than the previous one to give a series of 'steps'. When pressed, the edges will taper off smoothly into the garment without leaving a ridge.

Clipping. Except on very loosely woven fabrics the turnings of curved edges should be clipped as well as layered. This will prevent unnecessary bulk or lumpiness in the finished garment, and help seams to stretch and lie flat.
In the case of an inward curving seam, such as

an armhole, all you have to do is to snip at intervals with small, sharp-pointed scissors into the seam allowance at right angles to the stitching line, but being careful of course not to snip the stitches. For outward curving seams, such as collars, small notches should be cut at intervals from seam allowance. Again, be careful not to snip stitches.

Hems

There are various ways in which hems can be finished and stitched in place, but the following method is simple and quick to do, the stitching is virtually invisible on the right side of work, and it is suitable for most fabrics and garments.

Turn up hem to length required. Trim loose threads from raw edge, and neaten edge. Press the hem well, then run the tip of iron under neatened edge to take away any impression of stitching on the dress. Roll back $\frac{1}{4}$ in. round neatened edge on to right side. Very lightly catch the hem to the dress, using a single thread and sewing by hand. Pick up just a few threads of the hem fabric along the edge you have rolled back and a single thread of the dress fabric. Space the stitches so they are about $\frac{1}{2}$ in. apart, and leave thread loose between. This is called catch-stitching. As each stitch is worked, let hem fall back into position. Remove pins and basting. This method of stitching hems can also be used for stitching armhole and neck facings in position.

Buttonholes

Worked buttonholes. These may be made by machine or by hand. In both cases the buttonholes are worked after the garment is completed. To work by hand, first mark the buttonhole on the straight grain of fabric. Stitch around the mark, as shown in diagram below, circling at end nearer garment edge. Cut buttonhole on centre mark and overcast the edges. Now work buttonhole stitches over the edges working from right to left. At end towards garment edge, form a 'fan', as shown in the diagram. Make a bar at the end opposite the fan by taking several stitches across the end and working buttonhole stitches over the threads and through the garment cloth.

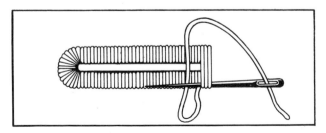

Bound buttonholes (tucked strip method).
Cut a straight grain lengthwise strip of fabric $1\frac{1}{2}$ in. wide and the total length of all buttonholes plus 1 in. for each buttonhole. Set seam gauge

on machine $\frac{1}{2}$ in. from needle. With edge of fabric strip against gauge, baste stitch the length of the strip. Repeat on opposite edge.

Fold strip to wrong side on stitched lines. Press. Baste-stitch $\frac{1}{8}$ in. from folds. Remove stitching on fold edges and cut strip into separate pieces the buttonhole length plus 1 in. With right sides together, place one folded edge exactly $\frac{1}{4}$ in. either above or below marked buttonhole line. Stitch through each fold the exact length of buttonhole. Fasten thread at both ends.

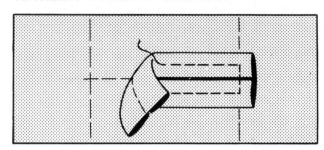

From wrong side, start at centre on marked line and slash through garment and strip to $\frac{3}{8}$ in. or $\frac{1}{4}$ in. from ends. Clip diagonally into corners. Turn strip to wrong side through slash, pulling the ends to straighten. On right side of garment, catch stitch together the bound edges.

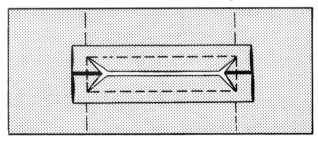

Place garment right side up on machine and fold material back so the end of strip and the triangular slashed piece can be put under needle. Back stitch across strips, ends and base of triangular piece. Repeat stitching several times.

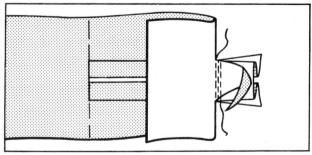

Pictured opposite: a quiet corner set aside for needlework. It is important to have a permanent place in which to work, with sewing machine in a comfortable position, and trimmings and accessories easily to hand.

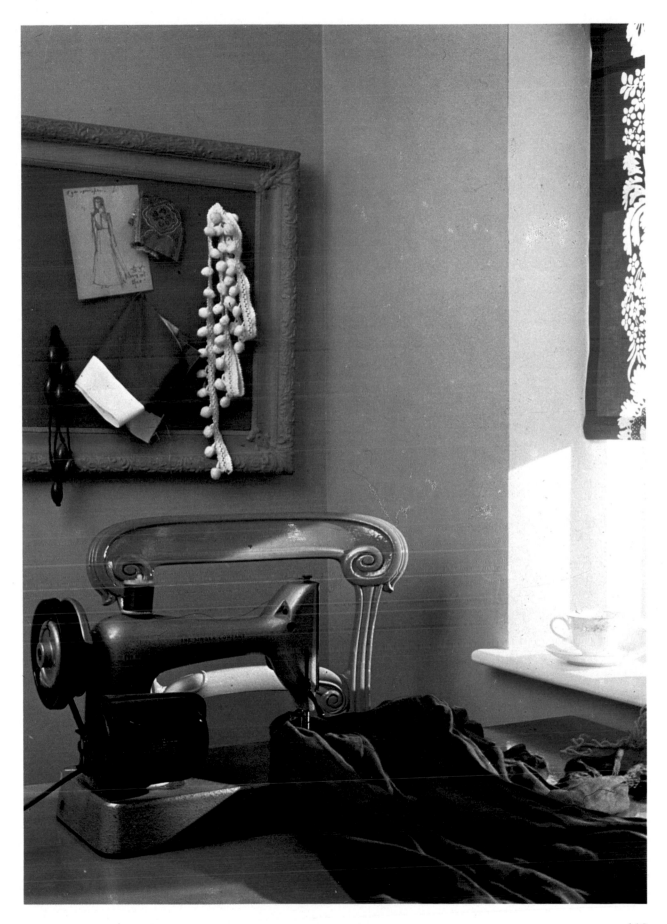

PAPER PATTERNS

Commercial paper patterns are ready for use. Normally they include full-size paper pattern pieces for the garment you are to make, full instructions for making up the garment, and a layout diagram showing how to place the pattern pieces on your fabric for cutting out. Follow the instructions and diagrams carefully — and you cannot go wrong!

Our garments to make, starting this page, are presented in the form of diagram patterns. This type of pattern is a replica in miniature of a full-sized pattern; you have to scale-up from the miniature diagram and prepare a pattern to the correct finished size, and then use this to cut out your fabric. Obviously this pattern preparation takes a little longer than if you are working from a commercial paper pattern, but it is not difficult to do.

The first step is to mark out a large sheet of strong brown or white paper into squares. If the diagram pattern you are following is given on a 1-in. grid, then mark out your paper into 1-in. squares. However if the pattern is on a 2-in. grid, or even a ½-in. one, then you must mark out your paper to correspond.

When your paper is clearly marked out in squares, copy the pattern as given on the miniature diagram on to your grid. Each of the squares on the miniature diagram represents one square on your paper. Copy the outlines and positions of lines, curves and angles in relation to the squares as accurately as possible. If you want to adjust the fitting of the pattern pieces, this the time to do it. For instance, if the diagram is given for a size 34 in. bust, and you are size 36 in., then add ½ in. to all side edges of both back and front. If you are a size smaller, then reduce the side edges by the appropriate amount.

If there are facings involved, these may be marked on the miniature diagram as shaded areas. Mark in the shaded area to your full-size diagram, then trace over these with tracing or greaseproof paper. Cut out all pattern pieces, labelling them if necessary so you know which part of the garment each pattern piece is for. Any markings or instructions on the miniature diagram should be transferred to the full-size pattern. A lengthwise arrow on the miniature diagram shows the direction of the lengthwise grain of the fabric. and indicates that the pattern piece should be placed in this direction on the fabric.

THE PATTERNS

Three-piece beach outfit
Also illustrated in colour on page 116

MATERIALS
For complete outfit (if made up in same fabric throughout) : 4½ yd. of fabric, 45 in. wide. **For wrap and suntop only:** 4 yd. of fabric, 36 in. wide. **For shorts and belt** (in contrast fabric) : 1⅝ yd. fabric, 36 in. wide. 2 buttons, each ⅝ in. in diameter. An 8-in. zip fastener. Petersham for waist band. Hook and eye.

FABRIC SUGGESTIONS
Our outfit is made up in Cepea printed cotton (wrap and suntop) and Tootals plain cotton poplin (shorts). Any cotton, plain or patterned, would be suitable.

SIZE NOTE
The pattern as given will comfortably fit bust size 34 in., hip size 36 in. To adapt pattern to fit your size, add to or subtract from the side seams of pattern pieces (see note on left); centre back length of wrap is 33 in.

TO MAKE YOUR PATTERN

The diagram on page 118 gives the pattern pieces you need. One square on the diagram equals 1 in. Prepare your full-size pattern on squared paper, following instructions opposite.

TO MAKE

Cut out fabric pieces, following cutting-out layouts below. Place pieces on fold of fabric where indicated on layouts (to avoid a seam at this point in the garment). All seams should be stitched $\frac{5}{8}$ in. from the edge of fabric. Unless otherwise stated, press all seams open after stitching.

Shorts

Stitch darts in back and front pieces, as indicated by guide lines. With right sides together, stitch centre front edges, then stitch centre back edges, matching notches.

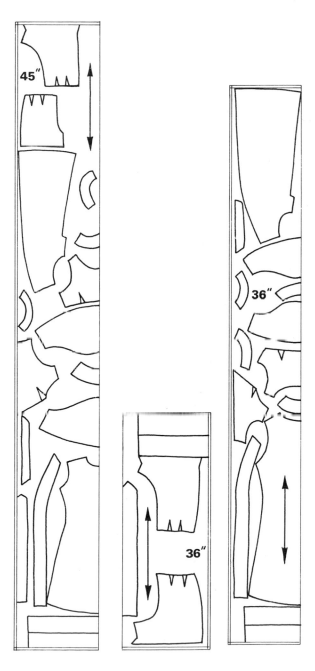

Right sides together stitch shorts back to shorts front at side seams, leaving left-hand side seam unstitched for 8 in. from waist edge. Stitch zip in position to this unstitched section of seam (see detailed instructions for stitching zips on page 129). Stitch inside leg seam. Trim and clip seam, layering if necessary. Cut a length of petersham your waist measurement plus 2 in. Right sides together, stitch this round waist edge of shorts. Press petersham to wrong side and secure with neat slip-stitches on inside of seams. Turn in ends of petersham level with side (zip) edges of shorts, and slipstitch neatly. Sew on hook and eye to fasten. Turn up hem round leg edges to length required, and catchstitch in place (see page 112).

Suntop

Stitch darts in back bodice, as indicated by guide lines. Stitch back bodice sections together at centre back edges, right sides together.

Stitch darts in bodice front sections, then stitch bodice front sections to bodice back, right sides together, at side and shoulder seams.

Stitch front facings to back neck facing at shoulder edge. With right sides together, stitch complete facing section to bodice, matching notches. Layer and clip seam, and turn facing to inside. Press well. Neaten raw edges of facings.

Stitch one armhole front facing to one armhole back facing at shoulder and underarm edges. With right sides together, stitch in place to one armhole edge of bodice, matching shoulder and underarm seams. Layer and clip seam, and press facing to wrong side. Press well. Neaten raw edge of facing. Stitch facings for other armhole in a similar way. Catchstitch facings lightly to inside of garment on seams to hold in place.

Stitch 2 lower band sections together along straight short edges, press seam open, then fold entire band in half length-wise, right side together. Stitch each pointed short end, following shape of point. Trim seams and turn band right side out. Right sides together, stitch band in position to lower edge of suntop, stitching through one layer of band only. Turn in seam allowance on remaining raw edge, and slipstitch neatly inside suntop, over seam just worked.

Make 2 worked buttonholes (see page 112) in the lower band, making the first buttonhole $\frac{1}{2}$ in. from centre front pointed edge on bodice right front, the second one 7 in. along. Make each buttonhole $\frac{7}{8}$ in. long. Sew buttons to lower band of bodice left front to correspond.

Wrap

Note. This pattern can be used to make an attractive light-weight summer dressing-gown.

Stitch darts in each front section, as indicated by guide lines. Stitch front sections to back section at side and shoulder seams, right sides together.

Stitch front facings to back neck facing, right sides together, at shoulder edges.

With right sides together, stitch entire facing section to centre front and back neck edges of wrap. Layer and clip seam, and press facing to wrong side. Neaten raw edges. Catchstitch facing to shoulder seams of wrap.

Stitch underarm seams of each sleeve. Right sides together, stitch each sleeve in position to wrap, matching notches and underarm seams, and easing sleeve as you stitch the seam as indicated on the pattern. Layer and clip seam.

Turn up hem at lower edge and sleeves to length required, and catchstitch neatly in place (see page 112). Open up centre front facings to stitch lower hem, then fold facings back in place over hem. Catchstitch facings to hem.

To make belt, stitch 2 sections together, right sides facing, along one short edge to form one long strip. Fold this strip in half lengthwise, right sides together. Stitch short edges at each end, then stitch long seam, leaving an opening to turn belt right side out. Trim seam. Turn right side out, press well, turn in seam allowance on remaining raw edges and slipstitch neatly to close.

Three-piece beach set, consisting of wide-sleeved
wrap, suntop and shorts – see page 114.

Left and above: *same basic pattern, made up in different fabrics, with different trimmings.*

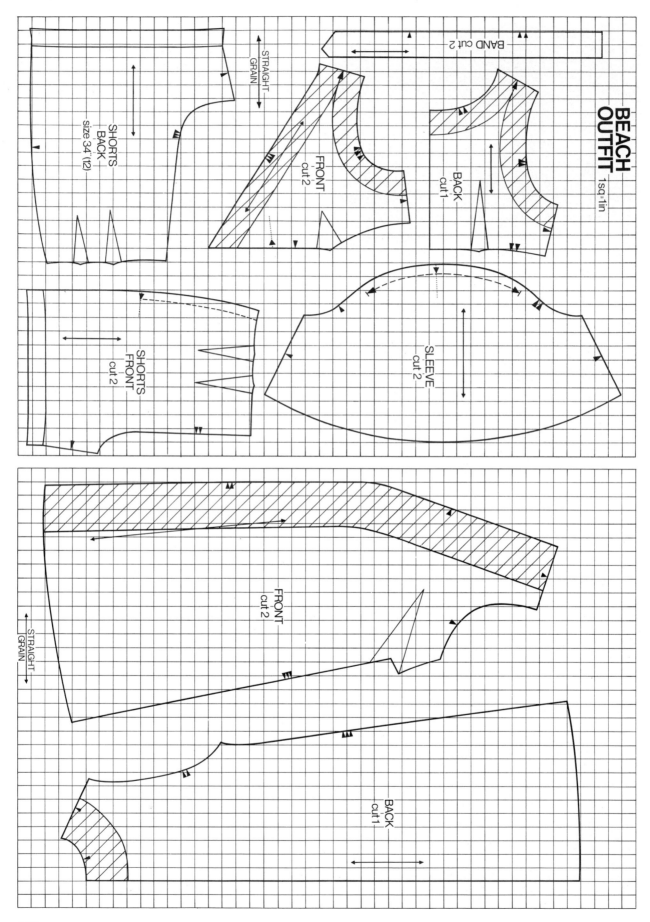

BEACH
OUTFIT 1sq=1in

BAND cut 2

STRAIGHT
GRAIN

SHORTS
BACK
size 34"(12)

FRONT
cut 2

BACK
cut 1

SLEEVE
cut 2

SHORTS
FRONT
cut 2

FRONT
cut 2

BACK
cut 1

STRAIGHT
GRAIN

118

Girl's cape and pinafore dress

MATERIALS

For cape: 2 yd. of fabric, 45 in. wide, or $1\frac{5}{8}$ yd. of fabric, 54 in. wide; 2 yd. of lining fabric, 36 in. wide; 4 round metal buttons; 1 hook and eye. **For pinafore dress:** $\frac{7}{8}$ yd. of fabric, 54 in. wide, or $1\frac{1}{8}$ yd. of fabric, 45 in. wide; $1\frac{1}{4}$ yd. of wide ric-rac braid, and $1\frac{1}{4}$ yd. of narrow ric-rac braid; a 9-in. zip fastener.

FABRIC NOTE

Our cape is made in Digoloom wool velour in red, with the pinafore dress in Digoloom washable wool in purple, trimmed with red ric-rac braid. Any good-quality wool fabric would be suitable.

SIZE NOTE

Dress and cape should comfortably fit a girl aged 5-7 years. To adapt the pattern add to or subtract from the side seams of the pattern pieces (see note on page 114); if necessary adjust the length as well; centre back length of cape is $23\frac{1}{2}$ in.; centre back length of pinafore dress is $22\frac{1}{2}$ in.

TO MAKE YOUR PATTERN

The diagram on page 122 gives the pattern pieces you need. One square on the diagram equals 1 in. Prepare your full-size pattern on squared paper, following instructions on page 114.

TO MAKE

Cut out fabric pieces, following cutting-out layouts below. Place pieces on fold of fabric where indicated on layouts (to avoid a seam at this point in the finished garment). For lining for cape cut side front and back sections and hood, following cutting line marked on pattern. All seams should be stitched $\frac{5}{8}$ in. from the edge of fabric. Unless otherwise stated, press all seams open after stitching.

Cape

Stitch shoulder darts in back, as indicated by guide lines. Stitch one centre front section to one side front, right sides facing, matching notches and leaving seams unstitched where marked on pattern. Stitch other centre front and side front sections in a similar way.

Stitch cape back to cape front at side edges, right sides facing. Fold each centre front edge back on to right side, so curved neck edges line up. Stitch from fold along neck edge for $1\frac{1}{4}$ in. Layer and clip seam, and turn right side out. Press.

Place hood sections together, right sides facing, and stitch right round curved edges (back and top of head). Clip seam and press open. Fold $1\frac{1}{4}$ in. round front (face) edges to wrong side. Baste to hold in place, then machine stitch on right side of work round entire edge $\frac{1}{4}$ in. from fold.

Stitch back shoulder darts in lining, and stitch lining back section to lining side sections, with right sides together. Stitch lining hood sections together, right sides facing, round curved (back and top of head) edges. Place hood lining inside hood, wrong sides together, and back seams matching. Turn in raw edges of lining round front (face) edges and slipstitch neatly in place. Baste neck edges together.

With right sides facing, stitch hood and lining in position to neck edge of cape. Do not catch centre front facing into the stitching. Press seam down. Place cape lining in position inside cape, wrong sides together. Turn in raw edges round centre front facings and lining, and slipstitch neatly to inside of hood. Turn in remaining raw edges of lining and slipstitch to inside of cape centre front facings. Turn up hems at lower edge to required length (open out facing sections) and catchstitch neatly (see page 112). Oversew facings in place along lower edge.

Place 2 tab sections together, right sides facing, and stitch right round edges, leaving a gap in seam to turn right side out.

continued on page 123

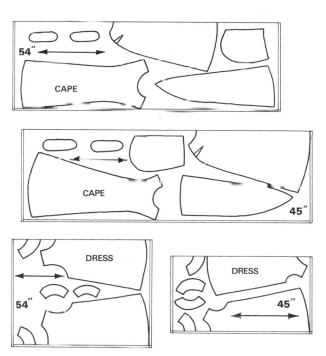

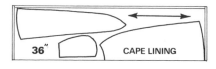

TO MAKE

Cut out fabric pieces, following cutting-out layouts below. Place pieces on fold of fabric where indicated on layouts (to avoid a seam at this point in the finished garment). Cut interfacing sections as shown, and cut lining sections as shown. All seams should be stitched $\frac{5}{8}$ in. from the edge of fabric. Unless otherwise stated, press all seams open after stitching. Stitch bust darts in coat front sections. Stitch back shoulder darts in back yoke section. Right sides facing, stitch centre back seam in coat back sections.

Stitch coat back to back yoke, right sides facing. Place right pocket facing in position on right pocket. Baste along top edge. Neaten opposite edge of facing. Place pocket lining in position on top of pocket, again right sides together. Stitch round top, right-hand side and lower edge. Layer and clip seams, and turn right side out. Press well. Catchstitch facing to lining on inside of pocket. Stitch left pocket in a similar way. Now place pockets in position on coat front, wrong sides of pocket to right side of coat. Line up side edges and baste. Slipstitch pockets to coat down inner side edge and lower edge. Fold each centre front edge back on to the right side, along fold line marked. On wrong side of coat, baste interfacing for centre fronts in position. Stitch neck edge from fold for $1\frac{3}{4}$ in. Layer and clip seam. Turn right side out. Press well.

Right sides together, stitch coat front section to coat back at shoulder and side edges, enclosing pockets in the side seams as you stitch, and enclosing interfacing in shoulder seams. Pin collar interfacing to one collar section, wrong sides together (this will be the undercollar). Stitch round all edges $\frac{1}{2}$ in. from edge of fabric. Layer and clip seam. Right sides together, stitch upper collar to undercollar round outside edges (leave neck edge unstitched). Layer and clip seams and turn right side out.

Stitch collar to neck edge of coat, with undercollar against right side of coat. Stitch through undercollar and coat only — do not catch upper collar into the seam. Press seam down, and baste unstitched edge of upper collar over the seam. On right front of coat, make 2 bound buttonholes (see page 112), positioning the first 1 in. down from neck edge, the second 10 in. below. Begin the buttonholes 1 in. from centre front edge, and make each $1\frac{1}{4}$ in. long.

Turn in seam allowance along neck edges of centre front facings and slipstitch neatly to basted edge of upper collar. If wished, work a line of machine stitching on right side of coat to enclose the buttonhole section on right front.

Stitch seam in each sleeve, right sides together, then stitch each sleeve in place to coat, right sides facing, and matching underarm and shoulder points as marked on sleeve pattern with underarm and shoulder seams of coat. Ease top of sleeve to fit, where marked on pattern. Layer and clip seam. Turn up sleeve hems, and hem round lower edge to length required and catchstitch neatly (see page 112).

To make lining: stitch darts as for coat, then stitch back sections together, stitch side and shoulder seams. Stitch sleeve seams, then stitch sleeves into lining armholes. Stitch hems round sleeves and lower edge.

Press well. layering and clipping any seams as necessary. Place inside coat, wrong sides together, and slipstitch in place round neck edge, to centre front facings, to sleeve hems and to lower hem. Stitch also round armhole seams.

Stitch hook and eye to fasten centre front neck edge, and stitch press stud to fasten front edges, midway between the 2 buttonholes. Stitch buttons to left front to correspond with buttonholes.

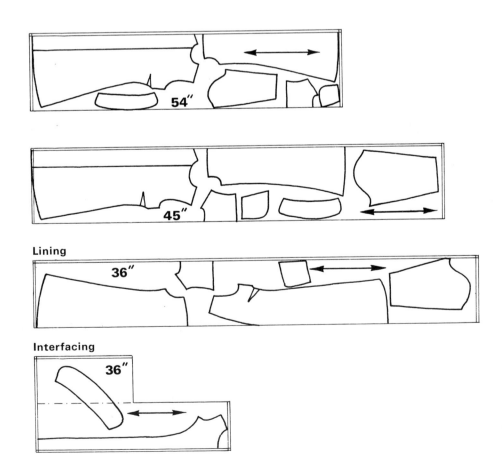

Lining

Interfacing

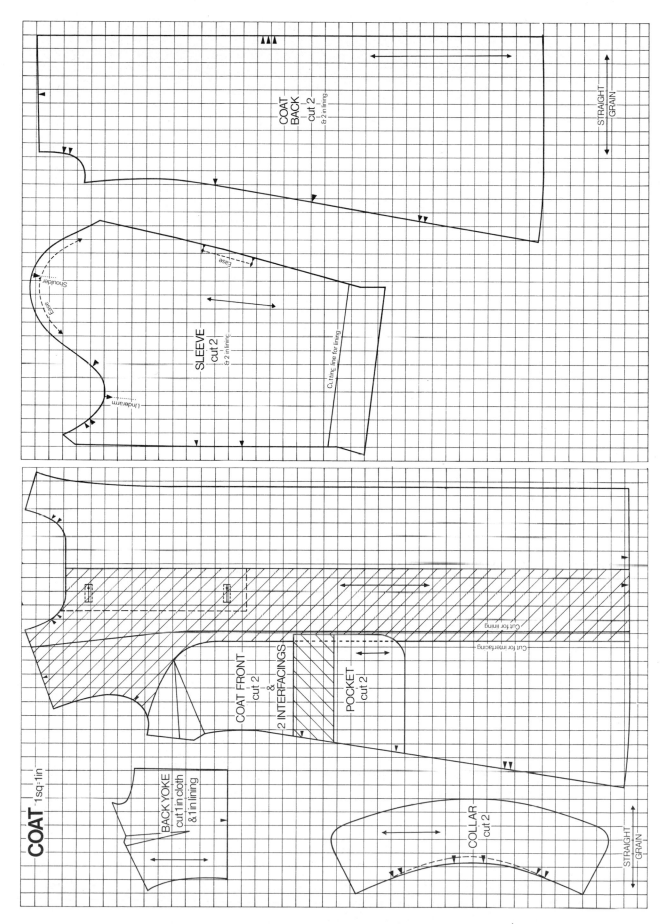

COAT 1sq=1in

COAT BACK
cut 2
& 2 in lining

STRAIGHT
GRAIN

SLEEVE
cut 2
& 2 in lining

Shoulder

Ease

Ease

Underarm

Cutting line for lining

Cut for lining

Cut for interfacing

COAT FRONT
cut 2
&
2 INTERFACINGS

POCKET
cut 2

BACK YOKE
cut 1 in cloth
& 1 in lining

COLLAR
cut 2

STRAIGHT
GRAIN

128

Two-way classic dress

This dress may be made either in normal length for everyday wear, or full-length for an evening or party dress. The everyday version is shown right, in black and white. The full-length version is illustrated in colour opposite.

MATERIALS

For short dress: $2\frac{7}{8}$ yd. of fabric, 36 in. wide, or $2\frac{1}{8}$ yd. of fabric, 45 in. wide. **For long dress:** $3\frac{5}{8}$ yd. of fabric, 45 in. wide, or $4\frac{3}{4}$ yd. of fabric, 36 in. wide; 4 yd. of lining fabric, 36 in. wide (optional); $\frac{3}{4}$ yd. of contrasting fabric for sash. **For both dresses:** a 20-in. zip fastener; a hook and eye.

FABRIC SUGGESTIONS

Our short dress is made up in Tootals printed Dicel, the long dress in Tootals printed Terylene voile. Any similar fabrics would be suitable.

SIZE NOTE

The pattern as given will comfortably fit bust size 34 in., hip size 36 in. To adapt the pattern to fit your size, add to or subtract from the side seams of pattern pieces (see note on page 114); centre back length of short dress 40 in.; centre back length of long dress $56\frac{1}{2}$ in.

TO MAKE YOUR PATTERN

The diagram on page 131 gives the pattern pieces you need. One square on the diagram equals 2 in. Prepare your full-size pattern on squared paper, following instructions on page 114. If you only wish to make short dress then follow hemline as marked on pattern, and omit sleeves, bow and contrast sash. The back neck facing is the same for both dress versions, but the front neckline and its facings are different. Follow appropriate line for the style you are making (i.e. high round neckline for short dress, low V neckline for long dress). For long dress, omit armhole facing section and tie belt, and use full length of the pattern.

TO MAKE

Cut out fabric, following cutting-out layouts on page 130. Place pieces on fold of fabric where indicated on layouts (to avoid a seam at this point in the finished garment). Cut 2 straight pieces of fabric, each 5 in. by 36 in., to make tie belt for short dress. Cut 2 sash sections for long dress from contrast fabric.

All seams are stitched $\frac{5}{8}$ in. from the edge of fabric.

Unless otherwise stated, press all seams open after stitching.

Short dress

Stitch bust darts in dress front, and back shoulder darts in each back section, as indicated by guide lines on pattern. Stitch centre back edges, right sides together, leaving seam open for 20 in. from neck edge.

Stitch zip fastener in position to this seam: baste edges together along seam line; press seam open.

Place fabric on working surface, so pressed seam is facing you. Place zip, right side down, over open seam with the slider 1 in. below the raw neck edge. Make sure teeth of zip are exactly in centre of tacked seam, then pin zip in place. Baste and remove pins. You can either machine the zip in position if you have a special zipper foot, stitching $\frac{1}{4}$ in. from teeth of zip all the way round. Or you can sew the zip in by hand. Use a single thread and work from right to left on right side of work, taking small back stitches and leaving a $\frac{1}{4}$-in. space between each stitch. Remove basting when zip is stitched in position. Press well. **

Right sides together, stitch front neck facing to back neck facings, at shoulder edges. Stitch facings in position to dress neck edge, right sides together. Layer and clip turnings, and press facing to wrong side. Press well. Neaten raw edges, turn in seam allowance on centre back edges and catchstitch lightly in place to tape of zip.

Right sides facing, stitch one front armhole facing to one back armhole facing at shoulder and underarm edges. Stitch to one armhole of dress, right sides facing and matching notches, and shoulder and underarm seams. Layer and clip turnings. Press facing to wrong side. Neaten raw edge and catchstitch lightly to inside of dress at seams. Stitch other armhole facings in place in a similar way. Try on dress and turn up hem to length required. Catchstitch neatly in place (see page 112). Sew hook and eye to fasten centre back neck edges.

To make belt, sew strips together at one short edge to make one long strip. Fold this strip in half lengthwise, right sides together. Stitch short edges at each end, and stitch the long seam, leaving an opening to turn belt right side out. Trim seams, turn belt right side out. Press well. Turn in seam allowance on remaining open edges and slipstitch neatly.

Long dress

If a lining is required follow cutting-out layout as marked, and cut out dress front and back sections only.

129

Make up dress, following making instructions for short dress as far as **.

Make up lining sections, if used, in a similar way. Place inside dress, wrong sides together. Turn in seam allowance on open edges above centre back seam in lining, and slipstitch neatly to zipper tape. Oversew lining to dress round armhole edges. Baste neck edges together.

With right sides facing, stitch front neck facing to back neck facings at shoulder edge. Stitch entire facing section in position to dress neck edge, right sides together. Layer and clip seam, and press facing to wrong side, over lining. Press well. Neaten raw edges, turn in seam allowance on centre back edges and catchstitch lightly to tape of zip. Catchstitch neatened edge of facing to lining to hold in place.

Right sides facing, stitch underarm seam in each sleeve. Run a gathering thread round top of each sleeve, as marked on pattern. Pin each sleeve in place to dress, right sides facing, and matching notches and underarm seams. Adjust gathers to fit. Stitch seam. Layer and clip seam. Turn up hems round lower edges of dress and of lining, also of sleeves. Catchstitch

neatly in place (see page 112). Sew hook and eye to fasten centre back neck edges above zip.

To make sash, fold one section in half lengthwise, right sides facing, and stitch long edges together, and the straight diagonal edges. Turn strip right side out. Pleat at unstitched edges as marked on pattern, and baste to hold in place. Stitch other sash section and pleat in a similar way. Now, with right sides together, stitch sash sections together at pleated edges. Stitch sash to right side of dress, stitching centre seam of sash to centre front of dress immediately below neckline, so sash forms an inverted 'V'. The ends are then taken under the bust and round to the back where they can be tied in a bow.

To make bow, fold fabric in half lengthwise and stitch down long side and one short side. Clip seams and turn right side out. Press well, turn in seam allowance on remaining open edges and slipstitch closed. Run 2 rows of gathering stitches down centre of bow, as marked on pattern, and draw up to measure 2 in. at this point. Stitch bow to dress front over stitched point of sash. Position bow so lower edge is the widest edge.

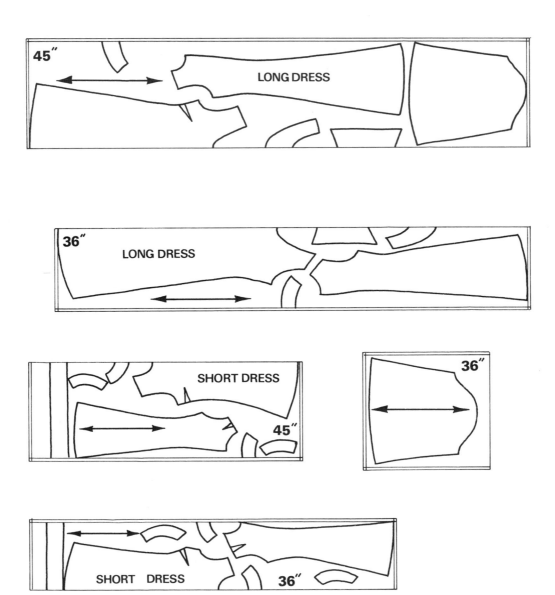

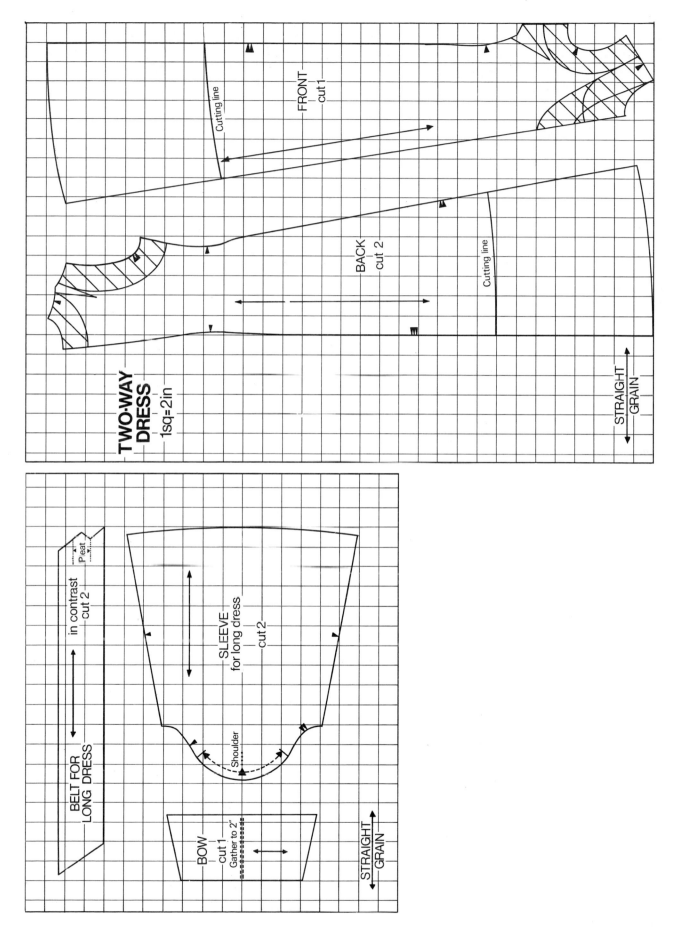

TWO-WAY
DRESS
1sq=2in

Cutting line

FRONT
cut 1

BACK
cut 2

Cutting line

STRAIGHT
GRAIN

BELT FOR
LONG DRESS

in contrast
cut 2

Peat

SLEEVE
for long dress
cut 2

Shoulder

BOW
cut 1
Gather to 2"

STRAIGHT
GRAIN

Boy's shirt and shorts

MATERIALS
For short and shirts in the same fabric: 1¾ yd. of fabric, 36 in. wide. **For shorts only:** ¾ yd. of fabric, 36 in. wide. **For shirt only:** 1⅜ yd. of fabric, 36 in. wide. A waist length of ½-in. elastic. 4 small buttons.

FABRIC NOTE
Our shirt and shorts are made up in Tootals cotton denim. Any mediumweight cotton would be suitable.

SIZE NOTE
Shirt and shorts should comfortably fit a boy aged 6-8 years. To adapt the pattern to fit a different size, add to or subtract from the side seams of the pattern pieces (see note on page 114) ; if necessary adjust the length as well ; centre back length of shirt 17½ in.

TO MAKE YOUR PATTERN
The diagram opposite gives the pattern pieces you will need. One square on the diagram equals 1 in. Prepare your full-size pattern on squared paper, following instructions on page 114.

TO MAKE
Cut out fabric pieces, following cutting-out layouts below. Place pieces on fold of fabric where indicated on layouts (to avoid a seam at this point in the finished garment). Cut one pocket section only.
All seams should be stitched ⅝ in. from the edge of fabric. Unless otherwise stated, press all seams open after stitching.

Shirt
Stitch back to front sections at shoulder and side edges, right sides facing.
Fold collar section in half lengthwise, right sides facing. Stitch along short edges at each end. Trim seams. Turn collar right side out and press well.
On each front section of shirt, fold centre front edge back on to the right side, lining up curved neck edges. Stitch along neck edge from the fold for ¾ in. Trim seam. Turn facing to wrong side and press well. Now place collar in position to neck edge of shirt, right sides facing. Stitch in place, only stitching through one thickness of collar, and being sure not to catch centre front facings into the stitching.

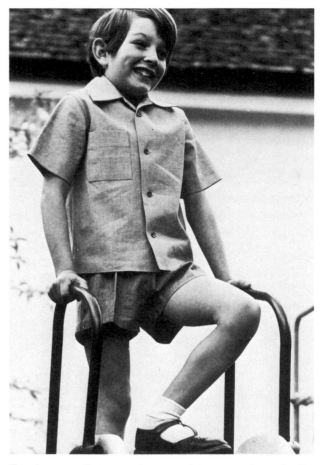

Turn in seam allowance along remaining raw edges of collar and slipstitch neatly to inside of shirt, along back of seam just worked. Turn in raw edges on centre front facings at neck edge and slipstitch also to back of collar seam. Neaten raw edges of centre front facings, and slipstitch shoulder edge to inside of shirt along seam.
Stitch underarm seam in each sleeve, right sides facing, then stitch each sleeve into shirt, right sides facing. Layer and clip seam. Turn up hems at sleeve ends, and lower edge of shirt (open out facings) and catchstitch neatly (see page 112). Fold back centre front facings and slipstitch in place to lower edge. Neaten all edges of pocket piece. Fold back one short end to wrong side, as marked on pattern. Position pocket on right front of shirt, as indicated on pattern. Machine stitch in place with a contrasting thread round side edges and lower edge. On left front (or right front is making the shirt for a girl) make 4 worked buttonholes (see page 112) positioning one 3½ in. up from lower edge, the other 3 at 3½ in. intervals. Begin each buttonhole ½ in. from centre front edge, and make each ½ in. long. Sew buttons to right front to correspond.
If wished work machine stitching in a contrasting colour thread round shoulder, armhole and side seams.

Shorts
With right sides facing, join centre front edges. With right sides facing, join centre back edges.
Join shorts front to shorts back, with right sides facing, at side edges, and at inside leg edges.
Neaten raw edges at waist, then fold to inside of shorts to form a 1-in. casing. Stitch, leaving an opening at one side seam to thread elastic through. Thread elastic through casing, and stitch ends of elastic together. Slipstitch opening in casing closed.
Turn up hems at lower leg edges to length required. Catchstitch neatly (see page 112).

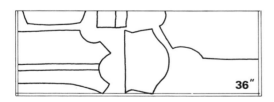

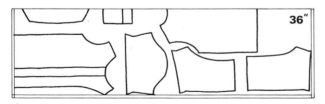

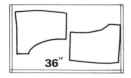

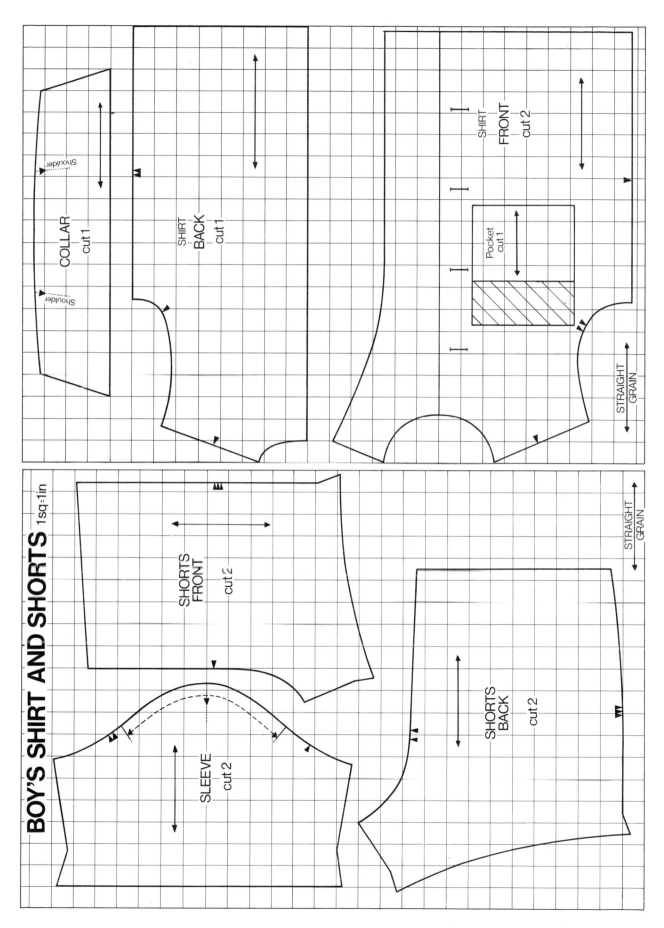

BOY'S SHIRT AND SHORTS 1sq=1in

COLLAR
cut 1

Shoulder

Shoulder

SHIRT
BACK
cut 1

SHIRT
FRONT
cut 2

Pocket
cut 1

STRAIGHT
GRAIN

SHORTS
FRONT
cut 2

SHORTS
BACK
cut 2

SLEEVE
cut 2

STRAIGHT
GRAIN

Chapter seven
MAKING SOFT FURNISHINGS

Soft furnishings provide the essential finishing touches to a decoration scheme, and are as important to a room as well-chosen accessories are to an elegant suit or coat. Although many of the basic sewing techniques as used in dressmaking apply to soft furnishings as well, in fact making soft furnishings demands a different approach — and a different set of skills. For one thing, you rarely work from a prepared pattern, and in order to determine the right amount of fabric to buy and to cut, you have to be something of a mathematician. The guide which follows will help you measure up and make successful curtains and cushions.

Choosing your fabric

It is important at all times to choose a fabric for curtains to complement and suit the particular room. For instance if you have a formal, traditional room, furnished with antique or reproduction pieces, and walls and carpet which show them to advantage, then you should choose a suitably formal fabric for curtains such as velvet, damask, taffeta or striped brocade. On the other hand, if you are decorating a modern study, with leather upholstery and hessian-clad walls, a matt fabric such as linen, wool tweed, coarsely-woven cotton, or even the hessian which has been used on the walls, would be more suitable. For a bedroom a dainty fabric is usually appropriate — printed cotton, glazed chintz, broderie anglaise or checked gingham. In kitchens, bathrooms and children's rooms, colourful and gaily-printed fabrics can be chosen.

Once the fabric type has been selected, by its very nature the fabric will almost certainly dictate the style of curtains which should be

Floor-length curtains in plain-coloured rayon complement the printed fabric used on walls and upholstery.

Another well-harmonised room setting – curtains are orange with a pink border to match the orange and pink walls.

made. Elegant fabrics are usually made up in a formal way as floor-to-ceiling curtains, with a shaped or draped pelmet, topped with a decorative valance, or for a really dramatic window dressing, finished with a swag ending with 'tails'. Also popular are pleated headings, pinch-pleated or cartridge-pleated, suspended from brass curtain poles or the 'invisible' type of curtain track.

Less formal rooms may need only sill-length curtains with a simple gathered heading concealed under a pelmet (wood or matching fabric), or a pencil-pleated heading on 'invisible' curtain track.

Basic rules of curtain-making

1. **Fullness.** All curtains should be generously full — there is nothing worse than limp, skimpy-looking curtains. If you have only a limited budget, it is preferable to buy a lot of inexpensive fabric than too little of an expensive one. The quantity of fabric required depends chiefly on the type of heading tape you intend to use, as these control the degree by which the curtain is gathered up. Usually there are leaflets available with the individual headings, telling you how much fabric to allow. If your fabric has a bold pattern, then you will also have to allow for matching the pattern – with a big pattern, this can amount to an extra yard on every second width.

If you are using the standard type of heading tape (as opposed to pinch-pleated tape, or any of the fancier varieties) allow at least one-and-a-half times the width of the curtain track for total width of the curtains.

Fullness chart

The chart below gives a rough guide to windows and minimum curtain widths. With bay or large windows it is usually better to seam the widths into two curtains, as this looks neater than a window divided up by four separate curtains. When joining widths, add the extra piece to the outer edge of each curtain. If possible use selvedge measurement as depth of turning, so no measurement is lost in curtain width.

Window width	Minimum width for each curtain	Minimum width for pair of curtains
18 in.	Single curtain only, 30 in.	—
30 in.	24 in.	2 x 24 in. = 48 in.
26 in.	30 in.	2 x 30 in. = 60 in.
42 in.	36 in. (cut from ¾ width of 48 in. fabric, or use 36 in. fabric)	2 x 36 in. = 72 in.
48 in. — 60 in.	One width of 48 in. fabric	2 x 48 in. = 96 in.
66 in. — 72 in.	60 in. (cut from 1¼ widths of 48 in. fabric)	2 x 60 in. = 120 in.
78 in. — 84 in.	72 in. (cut from 1½ widths of 48 in. fabric)	2 x 72 in. = 144 in.
96 in. — 100 in.	84 in. (cut from 1¾ widths of 48 in. fabric)	2 x 84 in. = 168 in.
108 in. — 120 in.	2 widths of 48 in. or 50 in. fabric	2 x 96 in. = 192 in.
		2 x 100 in. = 200 in.

Note. These widths are for standard gathered headings, if pleated headings are required, the curtains will need to be fuller. The exact fullness will depend on the heading tape chosen.

2. **Lining.** The appearance of most curtains is generally improved if a lining is added. The curtains are less likely to fade, they hang better and the life of the curtain fabric is prolonged. The only type of curtains which do not need lining are nets and the open-weave and sheer fabrics, although these can be backed with another lightweight fabric if wished. Some people prefer not to line glass fibre fabrics as they have a transluscent quality when unlined, but again this is a matter of personal choice.

The traditional lining fabric is a specially-woven cotton sateen, impregnated with a stiffener. The fabric is available in white, beige and creamy tones and also in a range of colours, so you can match your lining to your curtains. There are also specially treated linings which add to the insulation properties of the curtains. These insulated linings look just like ordinary curtain lining fabric on one side and come in a range of attractive colours, but the other side looks like a sheet of silver — heat rays bounce off this straight back into the room, so they keep it warm in winter and cool in summer. The silver side of the fabric is placed to the wrong side (back) of the curtain fabric when making up. Sometimes detachable linings are preferred to those permanently attached to the curtain fabric — for instance, if the curtain has to be dry cleaned, but the lining is washable, then it would obviously be more convenient if the lining could be detached for washing. Make up curtain and lining separately. Use curtain lining tape for the heading of the lining — the curtain hooks then go through lining **and** curtain heading tape together, thus locking the lining in position. This method is particularly satisfactory for shower curtains where you want attractive fabric curtains outside and waterproof curtains inside; or if you are lining a sheer or open weave fabric with another fairly lightweight fabric.

3. **Furnishing fabric only.** Never be tempted to use dress fabrics for curtains, however attractive and however much cheaper they are than furnishing fabrics. It is a false economy as most dress fabrics are not made to withstand the continual use curtains are subjected to, and the constant exposure to sun, condensation, and other elements.

MEASURING UP

It is essential that the window is measured correctly. If possible use a metal tape or a yardstick, as a dressmaker's soft tape cannot be held rigid and consequently the measurements might not be accurate.

You will need to allow for turnings at the top of the curtains and the hems as well as allowing extra inches for shrinkage. If you are using ordinary heading tape, an extra 3-4 in. at the top of the curtain is ample, but some pleated and other stiffened headings take more as they project above the curtain rail — the instructions given with the various heading tapes will tell

curtain. Allow 5-7 in. for hem and shrinkage on short or sill-length curtains, 7-9 in, on long ones. Add 1½ in. for each side hem, 1¼ in. for each seam, and remember to allow for overlapping if you have the type of track which crosses over in the centre.

Write each measurement down as you take it — ideally get someone to help you. Measure from the top of the curtain track to the sill, or the top of the track to the floor, depending on the length you want the finished curtains to be. Then measure the width of the window and the width of the curtain track, which may well project beyond the frame or window reveal.

Measuring the window

(a) width of window
(b) width of curtain track
(c) from top of curtain track to sill (short curtains)
(d) from track to floor (long curtains)
(e) inside window measurement (net curtains)

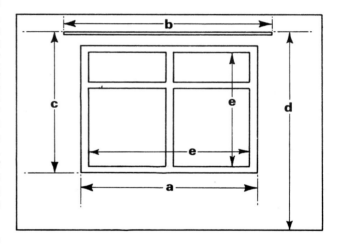

In badly-lit rooms, or where the windows are particularly narrow, it is a good idea to extend the curtain track at least 6 in. beyond the end of the window frame — further if you like. The curtains when drawn back will cover the wall and not the window, so no light will be cut out. Curtain poles in particular lend themselves to this treatment. If you intend to copy this idea, remember to add on the extra inches to each side of the window. When measuring, remember sill-length curtains should just clear the sill, this is particularly important with glass fibre fabrics which wear thin if they chafe against anything. Full-length curtains stay cleaner if they stop just short of the floor, so make them about 1-2 in. shorter than the measurement (d). Curtains should never hang midway between these two lengths and even when you are allowing for shrinkage, hems should be made at the correct length and the curtains let down when necessary. To calculate total yardage of fabric, multiply the curtain length, with hem and turning allowance, by the number of widths needed, adding on extra, if necessary, for pattern matching. If you are lining the curtains, you will need the same amount of lining fabric as curtain fabric (unless the fabric has a large pattern repeat and you have added on considerably more for matching), and if you are making a fabric pelmet or valance this must also be allowed for (see page 141).

When measuring for net curtains, as these are usually hung close to the glass, take measurement (e) both across and from top-to-bottom of the window frame. The top heading is usually 1-2 in., so a bottom hem allowance of 4-5 in. should be ample if you are using nylon or Terylene nets, but with cotton or rayon net, which might shrink more, add an extra 2 in. to the hem allowance. As net curtains are sheer, and are usually wanted as a screen, they look better if there is at least twice the width of the window in the fullness.

MAKING CURTAINS

First check that your fabric is perfectly straight by drawing a thread across the width, then cut along this line. Press the fabric to remove creases and measure down each selvedge the required amount for the first length and mark with a pin at right angles to the edge. Check the length by measuring back from the pins to the cut edge. When you are perfectly satisfied that you have the correct measurement (finished curtain length plus the allowances for headings, hem and shrinkage) draw across the fabric from pin to pin with tailor's chalk and a yardstick and cut across this line. If working with patterned fabric, check the pattern against the next length to get the correct match before cutting off the surplus. When you have cut all the required lengths, allowing for matching the pattern each time if necessary, trim away selvedges to avoid puckered seams, or snip the selvedge at regular intervals along the length. Do not treat the selvedge of nets or open-weave fabrics this way — leave intact. If you need more than one fabric width in each curtain pin the widths together, baste them, then machine stitch the seam (using a loose tension and a long stitch to avoid puckering). Press open the seams. If you only need to add part of a width, split the extra fabric lengthwise and join the widths together so the join comes nearest to the side of the window where it will not be so noticeable. If you are **not** lining

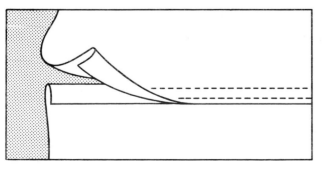

the curtains join the widths together using a flat fell seam, which is equally neat on both sides (see illustration at bottom of previous column).

Turn in hems (1½ in.) down the side edges of the curtains, place pins at right angles to the hem and press with a warm iron, baste then slipstitch by hand or machine.

For simple gathered headings cut standard curtain tape, in a suitable colour to tone with the basic curtain fabric, 1 in. at either end longer than the curtain width. Turn in the required amount of heading along the top of the curtain,

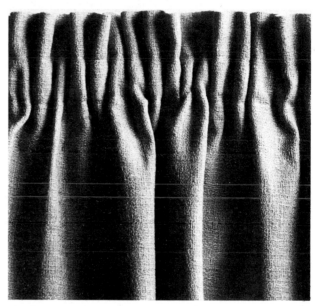

A simple gathered heading using standard curtain tape.

pin and baste in position. Turn in cut edge at each side of heading tape so it is the same width as the curtain leaving cord ends free. Place the tape in position on curtain so that it covers the raw edge of turning, and machine along top and bottom of the tape taking care not to catch the draw cords in the machine.

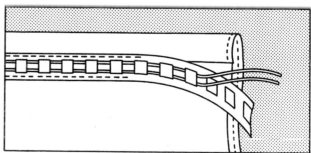

At the edge of the curtain which will be in the centre of the window, knot the ends of the cords together firmly, and from the other side, draw up the cords to gather the curtain up to window width, allowing an extra 1 or 2 in. Tie cords together firmly and tuck in ends behind curtain — do not cut them off as you must be able to loosen them for curtain washing.

Measure the curtains carefully for the finished length — then make the hem. It is often a good idea to pin and baste the hem, hang the curtains and allow them to settle for a few days, before pressing and completing the hems by hand. Small weights can be put in the curtain hem to help it hang more evenly, or you can buy lead-weighted tape which is threaded into the curtain hem and tacked at both ends to secure firmly. Insert hooks in the heading tape at regular intervals, turn over so the point of the hook faces downwards, and hang curtains by passing through 'eyes' of runners on the track.

FABRICS AND THREADS

Confusion exists over brand names such as Acrilan, Courtelle, Dralon — these are all synthetic fibres which may be used in furnishing fabrics, and come in a surprising number of weights, from open-weave nets to heavy tweed and velvet textures. These should be sewn with a thread suitable for synthetic fibres, but using needle and stitch according to the weight of the fabric. There are excellent multi-purpose threads available which can be used to stitch all types and weights of natural and synthetic fibres.

A Swedish semi-sheer acrylic curtain fabric featuring giant marigolds on a white background.

Fabrics			Thread	Machine needle no.	Stitches per inch
Fine	Voile	including Courtelle, Dralon, nylon and Terylene nets	synthetic or multi-purpose	9 or 11	8 - 10
	Silk			9 or 11	8 - 10
	Net			9 or 11	8 - 10
Fine/ Medium	Cotton	including fabrics with fibres as above	medium mercerised or multi-purpose	14	10 - 12
	Poplin			14	10 - 12
	Linen			14	10 - 12
	Satin			14	10 - 12
	Glass fibre			14	10 - 12
	Bonded fabrics			14	8 - 12
Medium/ Heavy	Brocade	including Dralon velvet	heavy-duty or multi-purpose	14	12
	Velvet			14 or 16	12

Handling open-weave fabrics

When sewing open-weave fabrics, a number of which are made in Courtelle, cotton, Dralon and pure wool, it is best either to make up the curtains by hand, or if you are machining to use a long loose stitch. When cutting the fabric, stick a strip of self-adhesive transparent tape along each side of the cutting line to prevent fraying — you can stitch through this and remove it afterwards. Side hems are not usually necessary as they tend to look too bulky, so leave the selvedges intact and try to avoid seaming the widths of the fabric unless absolutely necessary — if joining is unavoidable, make a very small neat seam and press well so it lies completely flat. Always let open-weave fabrics hang for a while to settle before finishing the hem.

LINING CURTAINS

If you intend to line your curtains with locked linings (those which are actually joined to the curtains), cut and seam together the widths of curtain fabric first, as previously described, then cut out the lining fabric about 3 in. shorter than the curtain, join the widths using a plain seam with ½ in. turnings — if the selvedges are tight, snip before pressing out flat. Turn up and stitch a hem 1-2 in. deep, along the base of the lining. With the top edges of curtain and lining together, lay the curtain out as flat as possible on the floor, and lay the lining over it, so the wrong side of the lining and wrong side of the curtain are facing each other. The lining now has to be locked into place by means of locking stitches — you will need to make two rows of these on a 48 in. wide curtain, three rows on a 1½ width and so on. For a single width curtain turn back a third of the lining from one edge (see diagrams at top of next page) and work a row of long, loose blanket stitches down the fold making stitches about 4 in. apart (2 in. for velvet). Take care that stitches do not show on the right side of the curtain. Finish a few inches above the lower edge of the lining to allow for the hem. To work the second row of locking stitches, turn back a third of the lining from the other edge and lock in a similar way. If you need more than two rows of locking stitches because

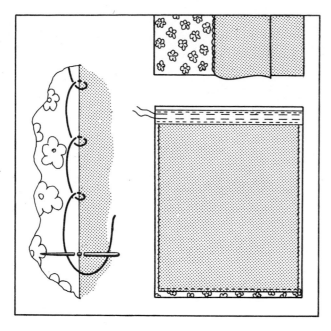

stitched end of the tape overlapping the lining by about 1 in. and pin carefully in position. Turn under the surplus inch so that the fold is in line with the wide edge of the lining. Machine the top edges of the turned-under tape together. Continue stitching along the folded edge and along the bottom edge of the tape keeping the top of the lining enclosed in the double 'skirt'. The underside is slightly longer than the corded side so stitching will not miss even though you are sewing unseen. Finish the other edge of the tape in the same way as the first, but leave the ends of the cord free for pulling up to pleat the lining as wished. Pull up the cords to pleat the lining to the required width — remember detachable linings should be slightly narrower than the curtains. Even out the fullness with your hand and tie the surplus cord neatly.

To attach the lining to the curtain, insert the stem of a hook through a buttonhole in the top edge of the lining tape and then through a pocket in the curtain tape, before turning over to its final position. Continue until all hooks are inserted, then suspend from track with the same hooks.

Hooking the lining in position to the lining tape.

NET CURTAINS

A variety of crisp yet delicate fabrics can be used for making net curtains, but if you choose Courtelle, Terylene or nylon, the fabric must be stitched with nylon thread or multi-purpose thread, and if the curtains are to be track hung, the heading tape should be Terylene.

As previously mentioned, net curtains should be generously full, at least twice the width of the window. If possible try not to seam the widths — some nets are very wide, up to 118 in., but if seaming is unavoidable use very narrow

the curtain is wider, fold curtain in half and lock stitch down the centre, then fold right-hand side in half and lock stitch down centre. Do the same with the left-hand side. Turn up, baste, press and stitch the curtain hems, and stitch the lining hems. Make single turnings about 1½ in. wide along the side edges of the curtains, press and baste. Turn in the lining edge so the fold lies ½-¾ in. inside the curtain edge, pin, baste if necessary, and then slipstitch the lining to the curtain taking care no stitches show on the right side and press.

From each bottom curtain corner measure upwards to correct finished length, mark with pins and draw a line across with tailors' chalk and a yardstick. Turn in both curtain and lining tops on to the wrong side along this line ready to stitch the heading tape in position. At this stage it is important to make sure that the lining and curtain fabric are as flat as possible, otherwise the curtain could look slightly crooked when hung. Now finish with curtain heading tape (see page 137) in a similar way as for unlined curtains except you will be sewing through five thicknesses with the tape, and of course will not be covering any raw edge of curtain turning. If this multiple thickness is too bulky you can trim off the lining to reach only up to the curtain fold. If you prefer to make detachable linings, use the special curtain lining tape. Make up the curtain lining with side and bottom hems, joining widths where necessary, but leave the top edge unfinished. At the left-hand side of the lining tape pull out about 1½ in. of draw cord and knot the ends. Trim the surplus tape to within ¼ in. of the point where the cord actually enters the tape. Turn under one end including knotted cords, and stitch across the folded edge to neaten. With the right side of the lining and cord side of the tape towards you, slip the top raw edge of the lining between the two 'skirts' of the tape, with the

French seams. Turn raw edges under the exact width of their hems, otherwise the curtains can look bulky in the sunlight. Use a fine needle and 8-10 stitches per inch and if the net shows any tendency to catch in the machine, put tissue paper on the stitching line and tear away when the seaming is finished.

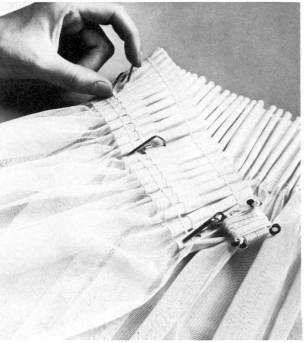

Deep gathered heading tape is available which is specially suitable for net curtains.

There is also a heading tape to give pinch pleats for nets and sheers.

The simplest type of net curtain to make is the gathered one which is held by a curtain wire at the top and the lower edge left free, although if preferred the curtain can be held with a wire at the bottom as well. Turn down the top edge and stitch neatly with the raw edge turned in, then make a second row of stitching above this to form the 'easer' to hold the curtain wire — hang the curtain and check the length before completing the hem or making the 'easer' for the bottom wire. If heading tape is used sew in place with synthetic thread, and if hooks are being used in conjunction with the tape, choose either the clear nylon variety or white plastic.

Cross-over nets

Use ready-frilled net for cross-over curtains and work out the amount of fabric required by measuring as follows: fix one end of a long tape two-thirds of the way across the track and loop to the side frame at the height you prefer, letting the free end fall to sill or floor. This gives the length for the looped side of the curtain (A). Measure the straight side from track to sill or floor (B). Add on at least 9 in. for hems and headings and allow at least 1½ the full width of the track for each curtain. Add measurement (A) to measurement (B) and cut as shown in diagram 1. If the material has a right or wrong side or a one-way pattern, double the long measurement (A) and cut as diagram

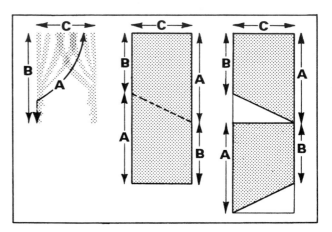

Use a heading tape suitable for net curtains and either head each curtain separately or over-lap the pair of curtains the correct amount, fold the top edge double right across both curtains and finish with one piece of Terylene tape to the correct width. Draw up to pleat the heading. Pretty tie-backs can be made from the extra fabric, sew Terylene tape along the edge of a strip of fabric and draw up. Insert small rings in the pockets at each end of the tape and slip the rings over small hooks at each side of the window.

TOP TREATMENTS

There are a variety of heading tapes available, usually a little more expensive than the standard tape, which will form your curtain tops into decorative pleats. Pencil pleats or cartridge pleats can be made by pulling up two drawcords in the curtain tape to give an evenly fluted heading; they are used in conjunction with ordinary hooks. Pinch pleats can be made by inserting special pleater hooks into the pockets of the curtain heading tape to give single, double or triple pleats. For a triple pleated heading, it is possible to buy a tape which is used with ordinary hooks; when the drawcords are pulled they lock at regular intervals to give a triple pleat with a 3 in. space between. These decorative heading tapes are sewn in place in a similar way as for the standard tape.

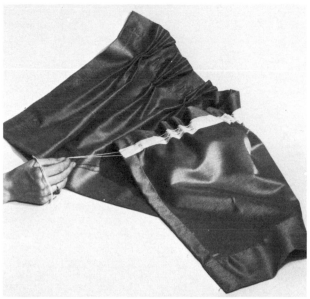

Just pull strings – and this 'magic' tape automatically pleats and spaces your curtains into triple pinch pleats.

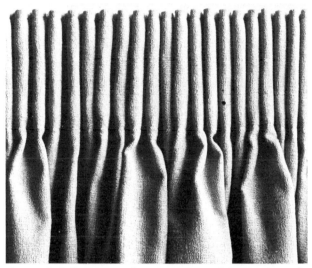

A special deep curtain tape gives this version of the standard gathered heading.

Calculating the fabric

Because pleated headings gather up more fabric than the standard heading, it is necessary to increase total quantity of curtain fabric. For a pencil-pleated heading allow at least $2\frac{1}{4}$ times the width of the curtain track, plus allowance for seams and turnings. For pinch pleats the amounts needed will depend on whether you want single, double or triple pleats. The following chart shows the measurement single width curtains reduce down to when pleated. Work out the amount of fabric widths you will require by dividing the track length by the pleated width, going to the next full width if it does not divide evenly.

Pinch Pleat Conversion Chart

	Triple pleats	Double pleats	Single pleats
48″ fabric pleats down to	22½″ (5 hooks)	24″ (7 hooks)	26″ (9 hooks)
54″ fabric pleats down to	22¾″ (6 hooks)	26″ (8 hooks)	29″ (10 hooks)
72″ fabric pleats down to	32″ (8 hooks)	38″ (10 hooks)	39″ (14 hooks)

Fabric pelmets

A fabric pelmet may be made in the same fabric as the curtain, or in a contrasting one, if preferred. The fabric for a pelmet should be cut across the width, not down the length; if necessary, join widths together to make required length. First decide on the shape and depth of the pelmet you require and cut a pattern from brown paper or newspaper. The taller the window the deeper the pelmet should be, but the usual depth is somewhere between 9 and 18 in. Pin your pattern across the top of the window to judge the effect and adjust if necessary. Use the pattern to cut out your fabric, allowing for turnings all round

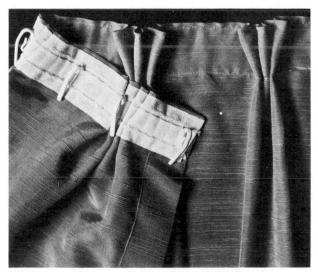

This tape gives a narrow pinch pleat and is particularly suitable for short curtains, sheers and nets.

(about 2 in.). Join the fabric if necessary and press seams flat. Cut stiffening (either pelmet buckram or a heavyweight interfacing) exactly the same size as the paper pattern. If the pelmet is to be lined, cut the lining the same size as the fabric, join seams and press flat. Lay the pelmet fabric, right side down, and centre the stiffening over it. If using buckram, hold down with weights away from the edges. Have ready a hot iron, water and a clean rag. Wet the rag thoroughly, damp the buckram edge about 2 in. all round and press down the turnings over the wet edges before they dry. The damp heat releases the glue which stiffens the buckram and holds the turnings in place. At the corners pleat them to lie flat. When the buckram is dry, lay the lining over the fabric and buckram, wrong sides together, turn in the raw edges of the lining with the fold slightly inside the pelmet edge and slipstitch. The iron-and-stick method cannot be used with interfacing, and this should be basted and stitched instead.

Pelmets can be trimmed if wished, with braid, fringing or any other decoration. Finish the top edge of the pelmet, on the lining side, with standard curtain tape but do not pull up the cords. Insert hooks every 4 in. to hang from the pelmet rail.

Valances

Valances are usually made to the same depth as a pelmet, but are like mini curtains. They can be pinch-pleated, gathered or pencil-pleated. Check the depth in a similar way as for a pelmet, then make up the valance as you would a full-size curtain, lining it if the main curtains are to be lined. Use the appropriate curtain heading tape to give you pleats or gathers, as required.

CUSHIONS

When your room is decorated, the curtains hung and the carpet laid, the room may still seem to lack personality. The addition of the right 'accessories' will usually add just the finishing touches needed. These accessories can tone with the colour scheme, but they can also contrast with it — providing accent colours. For example, some touches of vivid peacock blue and emerald green enhance a room decorated mainly in autumnal colours; very sharp pink can bring a scheme in blues and purple to life; splashes of bright coral or scarlet 'lift' a coffee-brown-cream room. One of the simplest ways to introduce these accent colours is to make your own cushions.

Fabrics

You can use almost any fabric for cushions — dress materials as well as furnishing fabrics. Silk, cotton, ticking, linen, poplin, dupion, felt, velvet, brocade are all suitable, but avoid very thin fabrics or those which are likely to crease easily. When buying curtain fabric it is worth buying a little more than you

need, so one or two matching cushions can be made with the extra fabric.

Simple cushions

The easiest way to make a cushion is either to re-cover an old one or to purchase a cushion pad filled with down or foam, and then make a cover to fit this.

Cut out 2 pieces of fabric, using the old cushion or cushion pad as a pattern, and adding ½ in. to all edges for turnings.

Right sides together, stitch fabric pieces together round three sides, if making a square or oblong cushion. If making a circular cushion, then merely leave a gap in the seam, so cover may be turned right side out. Trim seams, turn cover right side out, press well then finish the opening with a zip fastener, strip of hooks and eyes, press studs or a self-adhesive fastening. Alternatively, turn the raw edges in, press, baste and then insert the cushion or cushion pad into the cover, slip-stitch the opening and remove basting threads.

Piped cushions

A cushion with a piped edge looks more professional than a simple seamed one. Cut out the

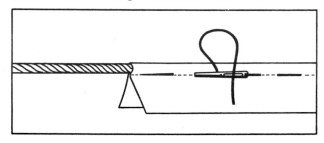

fabric for the cushion as described above, then calculate how much piping cord you will need to go all round the edge, plus an extra 2-3 in. Piping cord is available in a choice of thicknesses, to suit different sizes and types of cushions. To cover a medium thickness of piping cord, cut bias strips of fabric, 2 in. wide — this can be done in the same fabric as the cushion, or in a contrasting colour. Join the strips if necessary and press seams flat. Fold the bias strip round the piping cord and baste. Now make up cushion cover, as described for simple cushions, but sandwich the bias strip between fabric pieces as you stitch. Turn right side out and sew the piping to one side of the opening. Insert the cushion or pad and stitch the opening as closely as possible to the piping. Again, a zip fastener can be used to close the cushion if preferred

FINISHING TOUCHES

The right trimming can often add further interest to any piece of work — knitting, crochet, embroidery, macrame or sewing. Here are a few ideas for simple, easy-to-make trimmings, plus hints on keeping your needlework looking as good as new for as long as possible.

TRIMMINGS

Tassels

Cut a piece of cardboard the desired length of tassel. Wrap yarn around cardboard, tie a thread through upper end, cut through lower end. Wrap thread around upper part several times to hold tassel together.

Fringes

Yarn fringe. Cut a length of heavy paper the desired width of fringe plus ½ in. and as long as the part to which the fringe will be attached. Fasten the yarn to the paper and wrap it around the paper, laying the strands touching each other but not overlapping. Machine stitch across one long side about ½ in. from the edge. Cut through the strands on the opposite side. Tear away the lower part of the paper. Turn under and top-stitch the edge of the garment to the top of the fringe. Remove remaining paper.

Knotted fringe. Narrowly hem the edge to which fringe will be attached. Thread a large darning needle with 2 or more strands of the yarn. Turn under the edge to which the fringe is to be attached. Working from right to left, bring needle up through turned edge of fabric. Take stitches about ¼ in. apart, leaving loops of the desired length between stitches. When a sufficient number of loops have been made, cut them and knot the yarn of each stitch. Trim lower ends evenly.

Pompons

Method 1. Cut a large number of long strands of yarn and secure the ends. At intervals, tie a thread tightly around the strands. Cut through the yarn between these threads. Roll between the palms of your hands to shape a ball and trim evenly.

Method 2. Cut 2 circular pieces of cardboard the same size as required for finished pompon. Place together and cut a hole through the centre; the larger the hole the thicker the finished pompon will be. Wind yarn evenly around cardboard passing through the hole each time until cardboard is covered. Continue to wind yarn

round until hole is almost completely full. Break off yarn and cut through yarn and outer rim of cardboard. Tie yarn around centre between cards to secure and slip cardboard discs off. Shake well and trim if necessary.

AFTER-CARE

Knitting and crochet

Washing. Never allow a knitted or crocheted garment to get too dirty. Careful washing does not damage any fabric but when a garment is very soiled, normal use of washing agents will not remove all the dirt without rubbing and it is this rubbing which causes damage to the fibres. Make sure the washing agent, whether it is soap, soap flakes, soap powder or a detergent, is thoroughly dissolved in hot water, and then add cold water to reduce the temperature before placing the knitted garment in the solution. Always make sure that enough washing water is prepared to cover the garment completed.
Never boil any knitted or crocheted garment. The water temperature should be about 40 deg. C. (104 deg. F.), just hot enough for your hand. Do not use any form of bleach.
Allow the washing agent to remove the dirt. Do not rub the fabric. Gently ease the fabric in the washing water, but do not lift the garment in and out of the water as this causes stretching. All fabrics are more easily harmed or distorted when wet than in a dry state.
Take the garment from the washing water and gently squeeze to remove as much of the water as possible. Rinse the garment in at least three changes of warm water. The third rinsing water should be quite clear after rinsing the garment in it. If it is not it means that there is still some soap or detergent in the garment and another rinse is needed until the water is absolutely clear. Gently squeeze the garment on removing it from the final rinse and roll it in a clean dry white towel without twisting. This will absorb most of the excess moisture.
Spread the garment out flat on a clean towel and ease it into the correct shape and size. Allow it to dry slowly in the shade or in an airing cupboard.

Embroidery

Embroideries should be pressed as you go along as well as when you are finished a design. Damp thoroughly and place face downwards on top of a thick pad of material so threads will not be crushed. Choose iron setting according to fabric, and press well. Embroideries should be washed in warm water and soap powder. Always squeeze the article in the soapy water, then rinse well. Iron on wrong side when still slightly damp.

Needlepoint tapestry

A piece of embroidery worked on canvas must always be dry cleaned as the use of water would soften the canvas.